Sip and Stir

Sip and Stir

Joanne Meek and Shirley Woolley

Illustrations by Linda Jordan

South Brunswick and New York: A. S. Barnes and Company
London: Thomas Yoseloff Ltd

© 1973 by A. S. Barnes and Co., Inc.

A. S. Barnes and Co., Inc.
Cranbury, New Jersey 08512

Thomas Yoseloff Ltd
108 New Bond Street
London W1Y OQX, England

Library of Congress Cataloging in Publication Data

Meek, Joanne.
    Sip and stir.

    1. Cookery (Liquors) I. Woolley, Shirley, joint author.
II. Title.
TX726.M37 1973   641.6′2   70-39352
ISBN 0-498-01165-8

Printed in the United States of America

To Verlin & Tiger

—who would really rather
have been testing fish and steak

Contents

	Weights, Measures, and Quantities	9
	Introduction	13
1.	Beer	19
2.	Sparkling Wines	37
3.	White Wines	54
4.	Red Wines	72
5.	Fruit Wines	88
6.	Rum	113
7.	Whiskey	132
8.	Vodka and Gin	146
9.	Brandies and Liqueurs	160
	Index	187

Weights, Measures and Quantities

English Equivalent Measures

	American	English
1 cup of breadcrumbs (fresh)	1½ oz.	3 oz.
1 cup of flour or other powdered grains	4 oz.	5 oz.
1 cup of sugar	7 oz.	8 oz.
1 cup of icing sugar	4½ oz.	5 oz.
1 cup of butter or other fats	8 oz.	8 oz.
1 cup of raisins, etc.	5 oz.	6 oz.
1 cup of grated cheese	4 oz.	4 oz.
1 cup of syrup, etc.	12 oz.	14 oz.

1 English pint	20 fluid ounces
1 American pint	16 fluid ounces
1 American cup	8 fluid ounces
8 American tablespoons	4 fluid ounces
1 American tablespoon	½ fluid ounce
3 American teaspoons	½ fluid ounce
1 English tablespoon	⅔ to 1 fluid ounce (approx.)
1 English tablespoon	4 teaspoons

10 / Sip and Stir

The American measuring tablespoon holds ¼ oz. flour

Measures

1 gallon (U.S.)	128 ounces
1 half gallon	64 ounces
1 quart	32 ounces
1 fifth (4/5)	25.6 ounces
1 pint	16 ounces
1 cup (½ pint)	8 ounces
1 jigger	1½ ounces
1 pony	1 ounce
1 teaspoon	1/6 ounce
1 dash (1/6 teaspoon)	3 drops

Wine Bottles

	Servings
Jeroboam	34
Magnum	17
Bottle	8
1/2 Bottle	4
La Petite or Split	2

Glassware

Brandy Glass (3 ounces)	Collins Glass (12 ounces)
Champagne Glass (5-6 ounces)	Cordial Glass (2 ounces)
Cocktail Glass (3-4 ounces) (2½-3)	Highball Glass (6-8 ounces)

Weights, Measures and Quantities / 11

Jigger
 (1½ ounces)
Julep Glass
 (10-12 ounces)
Old Fashioned
 (4-6 ounces) (7)
Sherry Wine Glass
 (4 ounces)
Sour Glass
 (5 ounces)
Standard Wine Glass
 (6 ounces)

Introduction

Sip and Stir is a cook book that allows you to sip a little of your favorite drink as you cook. Everything tastes better with a little nip in it and it tastes even better if you are nipping while you cook it. This book is for the everyday cook and for the ones who need a little spice in their life. Cooking is a hobby the world over. Eating and drinking are pleasures enjoyed by all. This is a collection of recipes that use some form of alcohol, or if you would prefer, "booze." The recipes range from the exotic to the very practical. All are fun and we have included in the ingredients a little extra beverage for sipping while you are slaving in the kitchen. It is about time cooks received their just rewards. We feel that an occasional sip of wine, beer, or martini as you cook can only enhance the flavor of the dish.

Although we have included exact measurements, go ahead and add a little extra booze if you feel it is needed or you are working extra hard on a certain dish. If you can't tell the range from the refrigerator, this is a good indication that you do not need to add any more.

The recommended amounts to sip are for one cook. If two or more are cooking you will need to increase the amount of liquor considerably depending on your cooking partner. When testing the recipes, we found that when two cooked, more than double the amount was usually needed. Assistants tend to drink more. Observers should not be allowed as they increase the cost of the dish to such an extent that it is not practical.

To make it easier on the bartender, we have divided the book into chapters of related or specific beverages. If you are in a champagne mood, you won't even have to look at the rum section. This is a good way to use an open bottle leftover from a party or a good excuse to open a fresh bottle.

Each chapter contains a variety of dishes. We have arranged them in a menu planning order:

>Hors d'oeuvres
>Soups
>Salads
>Entree
>Vegetable
>Breads
>Desserts
>Miscellaneous

Miscellaneous items such as jellies and sauces are found at the end of each chapter.

We hope that the book will be just the beginning of your cooking with spirits and wine. After you've tried some of the recipes, try adding beer or wine to one of your favorite recipes. We think you will like it better. When your husband opens that next can of beer, pour a cup and add it to a meat casserole recipe and try experimenting. The alcohol content of all wines and spirits evaporates during cooking and only the good flavor remains and can be enjoyed by the entire family.

Sip and Stir

1
Beer

BEER FONDUE
ONION CRISPS
SPINACH-BREWED
 SOUP
SPRING SOUP POT
BAR-BEER-QUE
 CHICKEN
BASEBALL FAN'S
 SUPPER DISH
BEER AND LIVER
PORK CHOP AND
 NOODLE CASSEROLE

ROUNDUP STEAK AND
 ONIONS
TAMALE PIE
ALOHA BEANS
COMPANY POTATOES
FRENCH-FRIED
 ARTICHOKES
BREWERY BUNS
DELIGHTFUL DILLY
 BREAD
HOT CASSEROLE BREAD
SPANISH CORN BREAD

HARVEY WALLBANGER'S FAVORITE CAKE

Beer Fondue

This is a fondue dish the head of the family will ask to be repeated. It's a good main dish with a hearty salad, beer, and your favorite pie for dessert.

2 tablespoons butter
1 onion, finely chopped
1 bottle beer (12 ounces)
1/2 pound cheddar cheese, shredded
1/2 pound Swiss cheese, shredded
3 tablespoons milk
1 tablespoon cornstarch
5 slices bacon, fried crisp and crumbled
French bread, cut in bite-sized pieces

This recipe often takes at least a 6-pack of beer because fondue usually means that you'll have more than one sipping partner. If it is a hot day, have a few sips before you start. Melt butter and cook the onion in the butter until lightly browned. Stir in the beer and open yourself another bottle. Gradually stir in the cheese. Combine milk and cornstarch and add to this hot mixture. Stir until it thickens. Crumble bacon over the top just before serving. If you would like to dip something besides French bread, try small shredded wheat biscuits, apple slices, or celery.

Onion Crisps

You will find lots of ways to use these crispy bread squares. We cut them into small squares and use them for party snacks. Larger servings are good with soups, salads, or the beer that you are sipping.

3/4 cup beer
3 cups prepared biscuit mix
1 cup chopped onion

2 tablespoons butter
1 egg
3/4 cup sour cream
1 cup crushed potato chips
2 tablespoons chopped parsley

Open a bottle of beer and pour one cup into a bowl. Sip on the remainder. Add biscuit mix to the beer and stir with a fork. Pat the dough into a greased 9 x 9" pan. At this point you may want to open another bottle of beer for sipping. Sauté the onion in butter until light brown. Combine egg and sour cream with the onion and spread over the top of the dough. Sprinkle with crushed potato chips and chopped parsley. Bake at 450° for 30 minutes.

Spinach-Brewed Soup

Popeye's favorite vegetable has finally reached the soup pot, but even he would be surprised to see it combined with beer. We think you will like this different soup. Have at least two bottles of beer; one is for sipping.

1 package frozen spinach in butter sauce
1/4 cup cornstarch
1/4 cup water
3 cups chicken broth
1 cup beer
1 cup diced celery
1/4 cup diced onion
1 teaspoon soy sauce
1 hard-cooked egg

Cook spinach pouch in boiling water according to package directions as you sip on your beer. Make a smooth paste of the cornstarch and water and add it to the chicken broth and beer. Use canned chicken broth or bouillon cubes; 1 cube to 1 cup of water. Add spinach, celery, onion, and soy sauce. Bring the soup to a boil and simmer 15 minutes. Finish your beer and serve the soup in bowls garnished with egg slices.

Spring Soup Pot

This is an attractive dish that starts with a canned soup and a bottle of beer. Use it for a luncheon with a salad or as a first course for that "special" dinner. Pour a glass of your favorite brew and get out all the ingredients.

1/4 cup green onions, sliced
1 clove garlic, minced
1 tablespoon butter
2 cans condensed cream of asparagus soup
1 cup water
1 cup beer
1 cup cooked sliced carrots
1 cup sliced celery

Set your beer aside for awhile and sauté the onions and garlic in the melted butter until light brown. Add the asparagus soup, water, and beer. Cook and stir until well blended. Add carrots and celery and simmer for 15 minutes. This will give you time to finish your beer. Celery will still be crisp. Serve hot. I like to garnish this soup with leftover popcorn.

Bar-Beer-Que Chicken

Mom's gone shopping and Dad's cooking dinner tonight. This recipe is so easy it's bound to turn out good—he'll love sipping on beer as he cooks. You'd better be sure he has a 6-pack handy.

1 fryer chicken, cut in serving pieces
1 can beer
1 cup barbecue sauce
1 onion, sliced

Place chicken in casserole dish. Combine beer, barbecue sauce, and onion and simmer for 10 minutes. Pour over the chicken. Bake at 350° for 1½ hours. Sit down and have another beer. Your work is done.

Baseball Fan's Supper Dish

If Dad is watching a baseball game today, fix this hot dog and beer casserole and he will feel like he is at the ball park. He'll probably even volunteer to sip some of the beer for you. This is a nutritious dish for the whole family that contains meat, vegetables, and carbohydrates. Don't worry about the alcohol in the beer because it evaporates as it cooks, leaving just the good flavor. Open a beer and get out the hot dogs.

1 package frozen chopped spinach
2 tablespoons butter
1/2 cup chopped onion

24 / Sip and Stir

1 teaspoon salt
1/4 teaspoon garlic salt
1 cup beer
2 cups cooked rice
1 teaspoon Worcestershire sauce
1 pound weiners, sliced

Cook the spinach according to the package directions and drain. Have a sip of beer and melt the butter in a skillet. Sauté the onion until light brown. Stir in the salt, garlic salt, beer, rice, and Worcestershire sauce and simmer for 5 minutes. Arrange layers of spinach, rice mixture, and hot dogs in a casserole dish. You should have 2 layers of each. On the top push the hot dogs into the rice. Bake at 350° for 45 minutes.

Beer and Liver

This is a slightly different twist to liver and onions that we think you will like. Liver is one of the best foods we can eat; it provides a good source of vitamins and minerals. Check to see if you have enough beer for sipping.

1 pound sliced liver
3 tablespoons butter
1 envelope dry onion soup mix
3 tablespoons flour
1 cup water
1 cup beer
1/4 cup chili sauce
1/2 cup sliced celery

Brown liver in melted butter and drain on a paper towel. Add the onion soup and flour to the drippings and stir until well blended. Have a sip of beer and stir in the water, beer, and chili sauce. Add celery and return liver to the pan. Cover and cook for 20 minutes or until liver is tender. Serve on rice or noodles.

Pork Chop and Noodle Casserole

This is a rich, delicious casserole that the family or company will rave about. It can be done a day ahead of time and kept in the refrigerator. We think you'll like the flavor that the beer puts into this dish. It takes quite a bit of cooking time so you had better have a 6-pack on hand. It smells so good it will probably attract sipping observers to the kitchen.

6 loin pork chops
1 teaspoon salt

1/4 cup flour
1/2 cup butter
1 onion, chopped
1 cup milk
1 cup beer
1 cup grated cheddar cheese
8 ounces noodles, cooked
2 tablespoons chopped parsley

Dredge pork chops in a mixture of the salt and flour and save remaining flour. Melt 1/4 cup of butter in a large skillet and brown the pork chops and onion together. When brown on both sides, remove the chops from the skillet and set aside. Have a sip of beer and melt the other 1/4 cup of butter in the same pan. Stir in the remaining flour until well blended. Slowly add milk and beer. Have your beer handy for sipping as you stir the sauce until it thickens and begins to boil. Stir in cheese and remove the sauce from the heat. Grease a casserole dish and mix half of the sauce with the noodles. Top with pork chops and pour the rest of the sauce over the chops. Bake at 375° for 1 hour. Garnish with parsley before serving.

Roundup Steak and Onions

Everyone likes steak. You'll find the beer and onions enhance the meat flavor in this skillet dinner dish. Start with a can of beer. Pour 1 cup and set aside for the sauce. Be sure there is another bottle in the refrigerator because that doesn't leave you too much for sipping.

2 pounds round steak
1/4 cup flour
1 teaspoon salt
2 tablespoons oil
2 onions, sliced
1 cup beer
1 cup water
2 beef bouillon cubes
2 tablespoons flour
1/2 cup dairy sour cream

Cut round steak in serving size pieces and dredge in flour and salt mixed together; brown in hot oil. Add onion slices, beer, water, and bouillon cubes. Cover and simmer 1 1/2 hours or until tender. Remove steak and onions. Blend flour into the sour cream. Pour into the broth mixture that the steak has simmered in. Open the other bottle of beer and "sip and stir" until the gravy thickens. Pour over steak and onions. Serve with noodles or rice.

Tamale Pie

1/4 cup beer
3/4 cup corn meal
1 1/2 pounds ground beef
1 onion, chopped
2 tablespoons green pepper
1 clove garlic, minced
1 cup tomato sauce
1 teaspoon salt
2 teaspoons chili powder
1 1/2 cups creamed corn
1 small can pitted olives, sliced
1 cup hot water

Open your beer and pour yourself a mug full and pour 1/4 cup of the beer into a bowl; add the corn meal and set aside. Have a sip from your mug and get out the frying pan. Cook the meat until lightly browned. Pour off excess fat. Have another sip. Add the rest of the ingredients and simmer for 5 minutes. This is a good time to open another bottle if you are still thirsty. Add the beer and corn meal mixture and stir in 1 cup of hot water. Put in a baking dish and bake at 350° for 1 hour.

Aloha Beans

During the summer that I was in Hawaii, I really don't remember eating beans; but at the last luau we had, this was the first dish to disappear.

1/2 cup chopped onion
2 tablespoons butter
1 cup raw rice
1 cup pineapple chunks
1 cup diced tomatoes
1 can pork and beans with tomato sauce
2 teaspoons prepared mustard
1/2 pound ham, cut into strips
1 cup beer

Set down your beer and start working. In a large skillet cook the onion in the butter until brown. Add the rice and pineapple and continue cooking until the pineapple is browned. Add the rest of the ingredients; cover and simmer for 45 minutes. Stir occasionally as you enjoy your beer.

Company Potatoes

If you want to really impress your guests, try this easy potato dish at your next buffet. Prepare it in a skillet and serve it in your favorite chafing dish. The secret ingredient is beer; open a bottle and read on.

4 slices bacon
2 tablespoons butter
1 onion, sliced
1 clove garlic, minced
5 potatoes, peeled and sliced 1/4 inch thick
1 cup beer
2 tomatoes, diced

2 green onions, sliced with the tops
1 teaspoon salt
1/4 teaspoon pepper

Since the recipe calls for 1 cup, you're going to need an extra bottle for sipping. Pour 1 cup of beer and set it aside. Cook bacon in a skillet until crisp. Remove and drain. Add butter to the bacon fat and cook the onion and garlic until brown. Stir in the potatoes and lightly brown them in the fat. Have some beer and add the rest of the ingredients. Cover and cook slowly for 30 minutes. Finish your beer and stir occasionally. When ready to serve, sprinkle with crumbled bacon.

French-Fried Artichokes

I cooked this dish while living in Northern California where tiny artichokes are readily available. If you are fortunate enough to have tiny fresh artichokes, you will enjoy this recipe and it is fun to cook in a fondue pot. I have sometimes substituted canned artichoke hearts.

2 cups biscuit mix
1/2 cup beer
2 tablespoons parsley, snipped
1/4 teaspoon garlic powder
1 egg
1/2 teaspoon pepper
small artichokes 1 inch in diameter

Pull outer leaves off the artichokes and slice. Combine

all ingredients to make a thick batter. Dip artichoke slices in batter and then fry in hot oil. Serve immediately.

Brewery Buns

For your next barbecue surprise your guests with these homemade rolls. They are large so allow one per person, but you had better have extra for anyone who happens to be home while they are baking. The aroma will draw people to the kitchen and no one will turn down fresh hot baked bread. Have plenty of beer on hand for guests and sipping.

1 package dry yeast
1 cup warm water
1/2 cup dry milk solids
1 cup beer
1/4 cup sugar
1/3 cup cooking oil
1 tablespoon salt
5-6 cups sifted flour

Sprinkle yeast into the warm water and set aside. In a large bowl combine dry milk, beer, sugar, oil, and salt. Stir in the yeast mixture. Have a sip of beer and stir in 3 cups of flour. Beat until smooth. Stir in enough flour to make a soft dough. Have a few sips before you turn it out on a floured board and knead the dough until it is smooth and elastic—about 10 minutes. Place in a greased bowl, turning once to grease all sides. Cover and let rise in a warm place until double in size, about 1 hour. Punch down and let rise again for 45 minutes. This is a good time to open another bottle of beer. Punch down and turn out on a lightly floured board. Divide the dough into 2 parts and then each part into 10 pieces. Shape each piece in a ball and place on a greased cookie sheet. Let rise 1 hour and bake 20 minutes at 375°. Remove from oven and brush with melted butter.

Delightful Dilly Bread

Oh boy! Hot bread time is here again in the form of a cottage cheese and dill seed flavored casserole bread. This nutritious bread may disappear before it even gets to the table. Serve it with a hearty soup and a salad and supper is on the table. Set aside 1/4 cup before you start sipping on your beer.

1 package yeast
1/4 cup warm beer
1 cup creamed cottage cheese (lukewarm)
1 tablespoon butter or margarine
1 teaspoon salt
1 unbeaten egg
1 tablespoon instant minced onion
1/2 teaspoon dried parsley
2 teaspoons dill seed
2 to 2 1/2 cups flour

Soften yeast in warm beer. Combine warmed cheese, butter, salt, egg, onion, parsley, dill seed, and softened yeast in a mixing bowl. Add flour to form a stiff dough,

beating well after each addition. Cover and let rise in a warm place until dough doubles. Punch dough down. Turn into a well greased 8-inch round casserole dish. Let rise in a warm place until light (30 to 40 minutes). Bake at 350° for 40 to 45 minutes.

Hot Casserole Bread

This hot bread will be the center of interest at any meal. We serve it with a salad for a luncheon or it's great with a barbecue. It can be baked in a loaf pan or a 1-quart round casserole dish. I like it best in the casserole with a lid to keep it warm. If you are really thirsty, you had better plan on two bottles of beer because you will need 1/2 cup for the recipe.

1/2 cup chopped onion
1 tablespoon butter

34 / Sip and Stir

1 egg, beaten
1/2 cup beer
1 1/2 cups prepared biscuit mix
1 cup grated cheddar cheese
1 tablespoon poppy seeds
2 tablespoons melted butter

Pour a half cup of beer and set aside before you start sipping. Sauté onion in melted butter until light brown. Beat egg and combine it with the beer. Stir in the biscuit mix. Don't over beat; the batter should be lumpy. Add the onion and all but 1/4 cup of the cheese and mix together. Spread batter into a greased casserole dish. Sprinkle with poppy seeds and cheese; pour melted butter over the top. Bake at 350° for 25 to 30 minutes while you finish your beer.

Spanish Corn Bread

This unique hot bread is entirely different from our Southern corn breads. If you like foods on the hot side, it will soon become a favorite. Serve it at lunch with a salad or at a brunch with an omelet. It tastes great with the beer you are sipping. I hope you have another bottle in the refrigerator.

1 can cream style corn (1 pound)
1 cup biscuit mix
1 cup corn meal
1 egg, beaten
2 tablespoons melted butter

2 tablespoons sugar
1/4 cup beer
1 can green chilies, sliced (4 ounces)
1/2 pound grated cheese

Open a beer and set aside 1/4 cup to use later. In a bowl combine corn, biscuit mix, corn meal, egg, butter, sugar, and beer and mix well. Pour half the batter into a greased 8-inch square cake pan. Cover with chilies and top with grated cheese. Spread remaining batter over the cheese. Bake at 400° for 35 minutes or until brown as you finish your beer. Serve warm. Serves 6.

Harvey Wallbanger's Favorite Cake

You know it's a good cake if Harvey likes it. The first time I tasted his drink I wondered what the ingredients were. You will feel the same way about this cake. It always tastes like "more" to my family. You may be surprised to find that you will be sipping beer as you cook.

1 1/2 cups sifted flour
1 teaspoon baking powder
1/4 teaspoon baking soda
1/2 teaspoon each, cloves and allspice
1 teaspoon cinnamon
1 cup chopped walnuts
1/2 teaspoon orange rind, grated
1 cup chopped dates
1/2 cup butter
1 cup brown sugar

1 egg
1 cup beer

Sift all the dry ingredients together. Have a sip of beer and add the nuts, grated orange rind, and dates. Cream butter, brown sugar, and egg together until smooth. Add dry ingredients and beer alternately, stirring well after each addition. Spread batter into a greased 8-inch square pan and bake at 350° for 50 minutes.

2
Sparkling Wines

SHRIMP-STUFFED
  MUSHROOMS
CHAMPAGNE FRUIT
  COCKTAIL
SPARKLING
  RHUBARB SOUP
ORANGE-CHAMPAGNE
  SALAD
ORANGE-GRAPEFRUIT-
  CHAMPAGNE SALAD
SPARKLING
  GRAPEFRUIT SALAD
ZESTFUL FRUIT
  DESSERT SALAD
BARBECUED
  CHIPPED BEEF
CHICKEN EMERALD
CRABMEAT-ARTICHOKE
  OMELET
COLD DUCK-TOMATO
  PUDDING
GALA VEGETABLE
  CASSEROLE
SPARKLING CARROT
  CASSEROLE
GRAPE-CHAMPAGNE
  FLUFF
PEACH DUMPLINGS
PINK CHAMPAGNE
  SHERBET
KRAUT RELISH

Shrimp-Stuffed Mushrooms

This is an appetizer that will quickly disappear among your sipping friends. Maybe you have never bought fresh mushrooms because their price per pound is quite high. But if you do purchase some, you'll find that they are very light and really a good buy. Let's sip on champagne today.

10 mushrooms (2 inches in diameter)
1/4 cup butter
1 small onion, chopped
2 slices white bread, diced
1/4 cup champagne
1/4 teaspoon garlic powder
1 can shrimp, drained and chopped
1 tablespoon lemon juice
1 egg yolk
1/4 cup milk
3 tablespoons Parmesan cheese

Wash the mushrooms and drain on a paper towel. Remove stems and chop fine. Have a sip of champagne as you melt 2 tablespoons butter in a skillet. Sauté the chopped mushroom stems and onion in the hot butter for 5 minutes. Add the bread, champagne, garlic, shrimp, and lemon juice and cook for 10 minutes. Beat the egg yolk until light and stir in the milk, adding this to the hot stuffing mixture. Now is a good time to refill your glass. Melt the remaining 2 tablespoons of butter in a baking dish. Place the mushroom caps in the dish; turn them once in the butter and be sure the hollow side is up. Have a sip and fill the caps with the shrimp stuffing and sprinkle the tops with cheese. Bake at 350° for 20 minutes.

Champagne Fruit Cocktail

2 bananas, sliced
4 oranges, sectioned
1 cup whole strawberries
1 cup sliced strawberries
1/4 cup sugar
champagne

This is an elegant first course for a brunch or summer dinner. Prepare and chill fruits. Sprinkle with sugar. Serve in champagne glasses. Pour champagne over the fruits just before serving. This cuts down on your sipping time—but you can always finish it after dinner, providing there is some left in the bottle. Happy sipping!

Sparkling Rhubarb Soup

"Is it soup yet?" This time Dad not Junior will be checking to see if the soup is ready or if he can help you prepare and sip. This is a regal first course for brunch or dinner and is quite simple to prepare.

1 cup pink champagne
1 pint strawberries, sliced
1 pound rhubarb, chopped
1 cup orange juice

1/2 cup sugar
1 cup chopped orange sections

Find someone to remove the cork—you need only 1 cup of champagne in the soup so a sipping partner is recommended. He can run the blender too. In a saucepan combine the strawberries, rhubarb, and orange juice. Simmer for 10 minutes. Stir in the sugar and cool. Now you have time for a refill. Have your assistant get the blender out—he probably has it in the bar anyway. When cool, blend until smooth. Pour into a bowl and fold in chopped orange sections. Chill. When ready to serve, stir in 1 cup of champagne. Garnish with strawberries. Grandma's soup was never like this!

Orange-Champagne Salad

Instead of taking a pill, eat your vitamin C. This salad will provide a good source of the vitamin. The rich, fruity flavor will complement any meal. Pour a glass of champagne and read over the recipe.

1 package orange flavored gelatin (6 ounces)
2 cups hot water
1 can frozen orange juice (6 ounces)
1 cup champagne
1 small can mandarin oranges
1 small can pineapple tidbits
1/4 cup chopped nuts

Dissolve the gelatin in the hot water as you sip on

your champagne. Add the undiluted frozen orange juice and champagne and chill until slightly thickened. Stir in mandarin oranges, pineapple, and nuts. Chill and serve on lettuce leaves and garnish with fresh orange sections.

Orange-Grapefruit-Champagne Salad

This sparkling fruit salad can be used as a fruit course for a brunch or as a salad for dinner. It goes well with chicken or pork and will add a festive touch to any meal. Open the champagne and start sipping!

1 grapefruit, sectioned
3 oranges, peeled and cut into bite-sized pieces
1/2 cup orange juice
1/2 cup water
1 package lime flavored gelatin (3 ounces)
1 cup champagne
1/2 cup chopped nuts

Prepare citrus fruits and set aside. Sip on your champagne and combine orange juice and water in a sauce pan. Bring to boiling point and stir in gelatin until dissolved. Remove from heat. Pour into a large bowl and stir in champagne. Chill until almost thick and stir in citrus fruits and nuts. Chill until firm.

Sparkling Grapefruit Salad

This gelatin, although remarkably simple, is a family favorite. We make it whenever we have cold duck left over from a dinner or whenever friends give us a surplus of grapefruit. Open a bottle and let's try this salad.

1 package grape flavored gelatin (3 ounces)
1 cup boiling water
1 can grapefruit sections
1/2 cup juice from grapefruit
1/3 cup cold duck

After you have finished your first glass of wine refill and dissolve gelatin in boiling water. Drain grapefruit and reserve 1/2 cup of the juice. Add the juice and cold duck to gelatin and chill until slightly thickened. Enjoy your second glass of wine! When gelatin is slightly thickened, stir in grapefruit sections and chill until set.

Zestful Fruit Dessert Salad

This attractive gelatin dish can be used as a dessert or salad. It is chock-full of fruits that glimmer in the champagne base. We know you'll enjoy sipping on champagne as you work in the kitchen.

1 package lemon flavored gelatin (6 ounces)
2 cups boiling water
2 cups champagne
1 large can crushed pineapple
1 cup miniature marshmallows
2 bananas, cubed

Dissolve gelatin in boiling water. Chill until slightly thickened. Drain pineapple and reserve juice for the topping. Stir champagne, pineapple, marshmallows, and bananas into the gelatin. Chill until firm. As the gelatin chills, make the following topping:

1/2 cup sugar
2 tablespoons flour
1 egg, beaten
1/4 teaspoon salt
1/2 cup pineapple juice
1/4 cup cream, whipped
chopped pecans

Blend sugar, flour, beaten egg, salt, and juice. Cook until thick and cool completely. This gives you time for sipping. Fold whipped cream into cooled mixture and spread topping on gelatin. Sprinkle with chopped nuts.

Barbecued Chipped Beef

Here is a real western brunch dish that will appeal to the hearty eaters in the group. If your family seems bored with the usual breakfast foods, surprise them with this modern version of chipped beef on toast. Be prepared to cook it again soon. We know you won't mind sipping on some cold duck.

1/2 pound chipped beef
2 tablespoons butter
1 clove garlic
3/4 cup catsup
1/4 cup cold duck
2 tablespoons brown sugar
2 tablespoons peach jam

Biscuits:
1 1/3 cups sifted flour
1 tablespoon baking powder
1/2 teaspoon salt
1/3 cup shortening
2/3 cup oats
2/3 cup milk

For sauce, sauté chipped beef in butter. Stir in garlic, catsup, cold duck, sugar, and jam. Mix well. Simmer for 20 minutes. Sip and stir occasionally.

For biscuits, combine dry ingredients and cut in shortening. Stir in oats, add milk, mixing with a fork until dry ingredients are moistened. Turn out dough on floured board and knead until dough holds together. Roll out and cut into rectangles. Place on greased cookie sheet. Bake at 450° for 12 to 15 minutes. Split biscuit and top with barbecued chipped beef.

Chicken Emerald

Green grapes sparkle like emeralds in this champagne-sparkled sauce that tops our delicious chicken dish. Don't wait for a special occasion to try this entree.

1 package wild rice mix (6 ounces)
4 chicken breasts, split
1/4 cup flour
1/2 teaspoon salt
1/4 teaspoon pepper
1/2 teaspoon paprika
1/4 teaspoon ginger
1/4 cup butter
1 onion, quartered
1 carrot, cut diagonally in 1 inch pieces
1 bay leaf
1 cup champagne
1/2 cup cream
1 can green grapes (8 ounces), drained or 1 bunch fresh grapes

As you sip your champagne, read through the rice package directions. Prepare rice as directed; set aside in a warm place. Mix flour, salt, pepper, paprika, and ginger in a paper bag. Shake each piece of chicken in bag, using all the flour. Brown chicken slowly in butter. Add onion, carrot, bay leaf, and champagne and simmer covered for 25 minutes or until chicken is tender. Arrange rice on a heated platter. Place chicken on rice. Remove onion, carrot, and bay leaf—do not discard. I always save these to put in my soup pot.

Add cream and grapes to sauce and heat and stir until hot. Spoon sauce over chicken and rice.

Crabmeat-Artichoke Omelet

This is a gourmet's omelet for that special occasion. It is simple to prepare, yet elegant in ingredients. Serve it with muffins, fresh fruit cocktail, and hash brown potatoes laced with chives. If it's really a special occasion, you probably already have the champagne open and available for sipping.

2 tablespoons butter
8 eggs
1/2 cup champagne
4 ounces crabmeat
1 cup artichoke hearts, sliced
salt and pepper to taste

Melt butter in large skillet. Beat eggs with champagne. Be sure butter covers the entire bottom of the pan. Pour eggs into the pan and cook over low heat. Do not stir. As the omelet cooks, lift edges with a spatula and tilt skillet to allow the uncooked portion to go underneath. When the omelet is set, sprinkle half with crab and artichoke and fold over. Cover and cook about 3 minutes or until brown on the bottom. Serve immediately.

Cold Duck-Tomato Pudding

Grandma's stewed tomatoes never tasted like this hot tomato dish. You will only have to hunt as far as your refrigerator for cold duck, which comes in a bottle and is excellent for sipping.

1 box cheese crackers (6 ounces)
1/4 cup chopped onion
1/2 green pepper, diced
1/4 cup chopped celery
2 tablespoons butter
1/2 teaspoon basil
1/2 teaspoon salt
1/2 teaspoon Worcestershire sauce
1 can tomatoes (28 ounces)
1/2 cup cold duck

Pour a glass of cold duck to sip as you get out your ingredients. Crush crackers into coarse crumbs with a rolling pin. Cook onion, green pepper, and celery in butter until tender. Add basil, salt, Worcestershire sauce, and crumbs and mix well. Chop tomatoes into fairly large pieces. Drain off 1/2 cup of liquid and replace with the cold duck as you have a sip. Place half the crumb mixture in the bottom of a shallow 1-quart baking dish. Cover with half the tomato mixture; then another layer of each. Save a few of the crumbs to sprinkle over the top. Bake at 350° for 40 minutes or until the top is slightly firm. Serves 6.

Gala Vegetable Casserole

In the mood for a party? Open a bottle of champagne and celebrate as you prepare this party vegetable dish. Set aside 1/2 cup of champagne to use in the casserole.

1 cup fresh bread crumbs
2 tablespoons chopped parsley
3 zucchini, sliced
1/2 cup sliced green onions
1 can corn
3 tablespoons butter
3 tablespoons flour
1 teaspoon salt
1 1/2 cups milk
1/2 cup champagne
1/2 cup grated cheddar cheese

Just sipping on champagne makes cooking a party. Take a break and line a casserole with 1/2 of the bread crumbs and parsley mixed together. Sip on your champagne and alternate layers of zucchini, onions, and corn. Top with part of the bread crumb mixture. Melt butter and stir in flour and salt until well mixed. Add milk slowly, stirring all the time until it starts to thicken. Stir in champagne and simmer for 2 minutes. Pour over the vegetables. Top with the remaining bread crumbs, parsley and grated cheese. Bake at 350° for 35 minutes. Serves 6.

Sparkling Carrot Casserole

Here is a vegetable to sparkle a buffet dinner or please your family any night. It makes excellent use of any leftover champagne or it lets you open a bottle before the party.

2 eggs, beaten
1/4 cup cream
1/2 cup champagne
2 tablespoons chopped chives
1/2 teaspoon salt
1 tablespoon melted butter
2 cups grated carrots
1/2 cup grated cheese
2 cups cooked rice

Have a sip of champagne first; then combine eggs, cream, champagne, chives, and salt. Have another sip and stir in the butter, carrots, cheese, and rice and mix well. Pour into a 1 1/2-quart casserole; cover and bake at 350° for 20 minutes. Remove the cover and bake for 30 minutes longer. Serves 6.

Grape-Champagne Fluff

This light grape dessert is wonderful after a big meal and will satisfy the "sweet tooth" of your dessert lovers. You'll find yourself making it often when the grapes are in season or whenever you have some champagne left in the bottle.

1 envelope unflavored gelatin
1/4 cup cold champagne
3 eggs, separated
3/4 cup sugar
2 tablespoons water
1 tablespoon lemon juice
1 teaspoon vanilla
1 1/2 cups seedless grapes
small clusters of grapes, frosted

Soften gelatin in cold champagne as you take a sip. Combine egg yolks with 1/4 cup sugar. Add water and lemon juice and cook over low heat, stirring constantly until mixture coats a metal spoon. Stir in softened gelatin and vanilla. Chill until mixture thickens and stir in grapes. Beat egg whites until foamy. Slowly add remaining sugar as you beat until stiff. Fold into the egg mixture. Serve in champagne glasses or dessert dishes topped with grape clusters. Chill. Serves 6.

Peach Dumplings

Let's surprise the family with a real treat today. If you have a peach tree in your yard, this should be a weekly event during the peach season. You can use this as a breakfast fruit or for a dessert.

8 ripe peaches
2 tablespoons lemon juice
8 sugar cubes
2 tablespoons Grand Marnier
3 cups prepared biscuit mix
2 teaspoons grated lemon rind
1/2 cup milk
1/4 cup champagne
1/3 cup melted butter

By now you should be sipping on champagne. Dip the peaches into boiling water for 1/2 minute and then dip in cold water and remove the skin. Sprinkle peaches with lemon juice and carefully remove the pit from the stem side. Dip each sugar cube in the Grand Marnier and press 1 cube into the center of each peach. Have some more champagne and combine biscuit mix, lemon rind, milk, champagne and butter and stir until the dough comes away from the bowl. Knead a few times on a lightly floured board until smooth. Roll into a rectangle and cut 8 four-inch squares. Place a peach in the center of each square. Bring opposite corner of dough together and pinch in place. Brush with water and sprinkle with sugar. Place in greased shallow baking pan and bake 25 minutes at 350°. Serve warm with cream or hot brandy sauce.

Pink Champagne Sherbet

It sounds pretty, looks pretty, and tastes heavenly. Serve

52 / Sip and Stir

this gala dessert in champagne glasses and garnish with fresh strawberries for special occasions. You will like it and so will your guests. Enjoy sipping on pink champagne as you work.

1 1/4 cups sugar
1 cup water
1 1/2 cups pink champagne
3 tablespoons lemon juice
2 drops red food coloring
2 egg whites
1/4 teaspoon cream of tartar
1/4 cup powdered sugar
1/2 teaspoon almond flavoring

Dissolve sugar in water and boil for 5 minutes. Cool. When cool stir in champagne and lemon juice; add red food coloring to make mixture a pale pink. Freeze until almost set. In the meantime, sip some champagne. Beat egg whites until fluffy and add cream of tartar and powdered sugar. Continue beating until stiff. Stir in almond flavoring. When sherbet is almost set, fold in the meringue. Freeze until firm. Let sherbet mellow a few minutes before serving.

Kraut Relish

This is a dish with a variety of uses and it is a real man pleaser. Use it as a relish with pork and ham dishes or take it on a picnic and serve it as a salad garnished with tomato slices. There is a lot of chopping in this recipe but you will find it worthwhile since we will be sipping champagne.

1 large can sauerkraut, drained
1 1/4 cups sugar
1/4 cup champagne
1/2 cup vinegar
1/4 teaspoon hot sauce
1 1/2 cups celery, finely chopped
1 large carrot, finely chopped
1 green pepper, finely chopped
1 onion, grated

Pour water through the sauerkraut several times; drain and chop finely. Pour another glass of champagne and combine sugar, champagne, and vinegar in a saucepan and cook and stir until the sugar dissolves. Cool and add the hot sauce.

While the mixture is cooling, we will be sipping and chopping. Chop celery, carrot, and green pepper. Grate onion and mix all the vegetables together. Pour the cooled vinegar mixture over all. Cover and refrigerate for 24 hours.

3
White Wines

GARDEN CRAB DIP
CRAB CHOWDER
ORIENTAL SALAD
CABBAGE CALICO
CABBAGE AND
  MEATBALLS
CHICKEN ACAPULCO
CHICKEN SAUTERNE
CRAB ORIENTAL
CROWNED CHICKEN
GERMAN-ORIENTAL
  SURPRISE
SEAFOOD CASSEROLE

SEAFOOD SUPREME
SCALLOPS À LA
  BROCCOLI
WINE-POACHED
  SALMON WITH
  PRETZELS
WINE-TOPPED
  HAM ROLLS
DIXIE GREEN BEANS
HOLIDAY RICE
POTATOES ON THE
  RHINE
STUFFED ZUCCHINI

Garden Crab Dip

You better have a glass of wine before starting this recipe. It is so easy there's not much time for sipping.

1 cup cottage cheese
2 tablespoons white wine
1 can crabmeat
1 teaspoon horseradish
2 tablespoons diced green onions
1/4 teaspoon salt
1/4 cup sliced almonds

Put cottage cheese in the blender and blend until smooth. Have a sip of wine and remove the cheese from the blender. Stir cheese and other ingredients together. Place in an oven-proof dish and refrigerate. You're finished.

Before serving, bake 20 minutes at 350°. This is especially good served hot with garden fresh vegetables, such as sliced turnips, cucumbers, celery, carrots, radishes, and cauliflower.

Crab Chowder

This is a rich soup that is ideal for luncheons or a soup and salad supper. It is also a good way to get tomatoes into vegetable haters.

2 cups chicken broth
1/4 cup sauterne wine
1 cup crabmeat
1/2 teaspoon salt
1 cup diced celery
1/4 cup chopped onion
2 cups canned tomatoes
1 can cream of mushroom soup

2 hard-cooked eggs
parsley

Pour a tall glass of sauterne and get busy. Combine the chicken broth, wine, crabmeat, salt, celery, and onion and simmer for 45 minutes. While it simmers finish your wine and read the paper. Ready for another glass? Combine the tomatoes and mushroom soup in a blender and mix until smooth. Pour into the hot crab mixture and cook until hot. Garnish with hard-cooked egg slices and parsley. Whip up a salad, open another bottle of wine, and dinner is ready.

Oriental Salad

This salad is very different and a real man pleaser. Drink a glass of good white wine before you start because it takes only a short time to prepare, but it must be made 24 hours before serving.

1/2 cup vinegar
1 teaspoon soy sauce
1/2 cup sugar
1/2 cup white wine
1 can bean sprouts
1 onion, sliced
1 cucumber, sliced
1 can water chestnuts, sliced

Combine vinegar, soy sauce, and sugar and bring to a boil, stirring until sugar is dissolved. Pour in the wine.

Mix bean sprouts, onion, cucumber, and water chestnuts in a bowl and add the marinade mixture. Place in the refrigerator for 24 hours. Drain before serving. Garnish with tomato wedges. Serve leftover wine with dinner. It is delicious with sweet and sour pork, green beans, and hot rolls.

Cabbage Calico

This vegetable only takes a few minutes to prepare but you will have time to sip Chablis while it simmers.

1/4 cup margarine
1 large head cabbage, chopped coarsely
1/2 cup Chablis wine
1/2 teaspoon tarragon
1 teaspoon salt
1/4 teaspoon coarse ground pepper
1 can corned beef, crumbled

In a Dutch oven melt margarine and add cabbage. Cook uncovered, stirring occasionally, for 10 minutes. This is the time to sip! Add wine, tarragon, salt, pepper, and corned beef. Cover tightly and simmer 10 minutes or until the cabbage is tender. There should be enough liquid in the pot to serve with the cabbage. It's too good to throw away.

Cabbage and Meatballs

This orientally inspired recipe will become a family favorite. You may use any white table wine. We like it with a dry Chablis. You might like to sip on a glass as you read the recipe over.

1 1/2 pounds ground beef
1/4 cup mushrooms, chopped fine
6 water chestnuts, chopped
1 medium onion, grated
1/4 teaspoon ginger
1/2 teaspoon salt
1 tablespoon soy sauce
1 egg
3 tablespoons oil
1 cup water
1/2 cup white wine
2 chicken bouillon cubes
1 head cabbage

When you finish chopping and grating have at least 2 sips of wine; you are finished with the hard part. Mix the first 8 ingredients together and shape into meatballs. Cook in hot oil until brown on all sides. Drain the meatballs on a paper towel. Go ahead, pour another glass of wine. In a saucepan combine water, wine and bouillon cubes and simmer until cubes dissolve. Slice cabbage and arrange it in layers in the bottom of a large casserole. Top with meatballs and the wine sauce. Cook over low heat until cabbage is tender. This will take about 20 minutes. You have time for one more glass of wine while you cook the rice to serve with this dish. Now don't you feel good?

Chicken Acapulco

This Mexican flavored chicken casserole will be the hit of your next buffet. We like it because it can be prepared ahead of time. Chenin Blanc is an excellent sipping wine. Your guests will enjoy it with dinner. Buy two bottles.

1 fryer, cut in serving pieces
1/2 cup flour
1/4 cup butter
1 cup chicken broth
1 cup white wine
3 tomatoes, peeled and sliced
1/3 cup sliced stuffed olives
1/2 cup sliced celery
1 onion, sliced
1 green pepper, chopped
1 teaspoon salt
1 teaspoon paprika
1/2 cup Parmesan cheese

Dredge chicken in flour and brown in melted butter. Place browned chicken in large casserole dish. Add any remaining flour and the drippings from browning the chicken. Add chicken broth and wine and stir until it thickens. Have a sip of wine and peel and slice tomatoes and arrange around the chicken. Add olives, celery, onion, green pepper, and sprinkle salt and paprika over all. Have another sip and pour the wine sauce over the ingredients. Bake at 350° for 45 minutes. Sprinkle with Parmesan cheese and serve.

Chicken Sauterne

Total preparation time for this dish is about one hour, which allows ample sipping time between chores. It's a complete meal in itself. Add hot biscuits and a fresh fruit salad if you're having company. I usually allow one chicken breast per person but some men will want two, so be prepared.

4 chicken breasts
flour for dredging
3 tablespoons butter
3 tablespoons flour
1 cup chicken broth
1/2 cup light cream
1/2 cup sauterne wine
1 tablespoon dried minced onion
1 teaspoon salt
1/2 teaspoon paprika
1/2 teaspoon oregano
1 teaspoon Worcestershire sauce
1 package frozen green peas with onions
1/4 pound fresh mushrooms

Start with a glass of white wine. Dredge chicken in flour and brown in melted butter; when brown, remove from pan and stir in flour. Stir in chicken broth, cream, and wine and simmer until thickened. Add onion, salt, paprika, oregano, and Worcestershire sauce. Place chicken in a casserole, add uncooked peas and mushrooms. Pour sauce over all. Cover and bake at 350° for 45 minutes.

Crab Oriental

This is an oriental dish that all your guests will want to try. It is attractive and very easy to prepare. We serve it with rice and the Dixie Green Beans that you can find in this chapter.

1/4 cup olive oil
1/2 pound pork steak, cut in strips
1 clove garlic, chopped
2 tablespoons soy sauce
1 tablespoon sugar
1 teaspoon salt
1 1/4 cups water
1 cup white Chablis
3 tablespoons cornstarch
1/2 pound fresh crabmeat or 2 cans
1/2 cup green onions, cut in strips
1/2 cup celery, cut in narrow strips

This recipe requires a lot of stirring, so plan on a lot of sipping and start with a large glass of Chablis. Heat oil in large skillet and add the pork pieces and garlic. Cook and stir until pork is done—about 15 minutes. Drain off excess oil. Add soy sauce, sugar, salt, 1 cup water, and wine. Have another sip and mix cornstarch with 1/4 cup water to make a smooth paste. Add to your mixture and heat and stir until thick and translucent. Add crab, onions, and celery; cook for 8 minutes. Vegetables will still be crisp. Serves 6.

Crowned Chicken

This is a Sunday dinner special. The men will want second helpings of the dumplings which crown this regal chicken dish.

1 chicken fryer, cut up
1/4 cup salad oil
1 can cream of chicken soup
1 teaspoon salt
1 1/2 cups sauterne wine
1/2 cup fresh mushrooms
1/2 cup boiling onions
1 carrot, grated
1 can of biscuits
1 tablespoon chopped parsley

If it is a hot day, make a big wine cooler. This dish does take a little time. After refreshing yourself with a sip, brown the chicken in hot oil in a Dutch oven. Remove chicken and drain off oil. Have another drink and add soup, salt, and wine and stir until smooth. Add the chicken, mushrooms, onions, and carrot and simmer covered for 40 minutes or until chicken is tender. Remove from heat and arrange biscuits in a circle on top. Cover and simmer until biscuits are done. Sprinkle with the parsley and serve.

German-Oriental Surprise

This is a good recipe to cook in October during the famous German *Oktoberfest*. It uses a delightful light German wine in a rice casserole dish. This wine-rice dish is excellent with chicken or fish.

Start with a small glass of wine—isn't it good? You'd better set aside 1 cup of the wine now or you may drink it all.

1 pound pork sausage
1 bunch celery, sliced
2 onions, sliced
1 green pepper, diced
2 envelopes dry chicken noodle soup
5 cups boiling water
1 1/2 cups long grain uncooked rice
1 1/2 cups almonds
1 cup Riesling German wine

Cook the sausage until brown and pour off fat. Save 2 tablespoons. Add sausage, celery, onions, and green pepper. Cook for 10 minutes. Cook the soup in 5 cups of boiling water for 5 minutes. Add the cooked vegetables. Have a sip of wine and stir in the rice, meat, and almonds. Now add 1 cup of wine. Pour into a baking dish and cover. If you don't have a lid use foil. Bake at 375° for 1 1/2 hours. This gives you plenty of time to sit down and enjoy the rest of the bottle.

Seafood Casserole

Pour yourself a glass of wine while you prepare the wild rice—follow the directions on the box. It takes a little time, but you will find it well worth the effort. Now you are ready for a second glass as you quickly put the casserole together.

1/2 cup wild rice
1/2 cup rice
1 onion, diced
1/2 cup butter
1/4 cup flour
1/2 cup white wine
1 cup chicken broth
1 1/2 cups fresh mushrooms
1 can crabmeat
1 can large shrimp
1 1/2 teaspoons salt
1/2 cup slivered almonds

Cook the wild rice and plain rice and set aside—use leftovers if you have them. Relax with a glass of wine and proceed by browning the onion in the melted butter. Stir in the flour and gradually add wine and chicken broth to make a sauce. Stir until it thickens. This gives you a chance for a sip or two. Add the mushrooms (slice some and leave some whole), crab, shrimp, and salt. Simmer for about 10 minutes. Pour over the two rices mixed together in a casserole dish. Sprinkle with almonds. Bake at 350° for 45 minutes. Garnish with parsley. Sit down and enjoy the rest of your wine.

Seafood Supreme

2 1/2 cups medium white sauce

1/2 cup sauterne
1 1/2 cups celery, cut diagonally
1/2 cup mushrooms
2 tablespoons salad oil
1/4 cup minced green onions
1/2 cup water chestnuts
1/2 cup chopped green pepper
1 1/4 cups crabmeat
1 cup shrimp
1 can (3 ounces) Chinese fried noodles
1/4 cup slivered almonds

Pour yourself a glass of sauterne. Make a medium white sauce and add 1/2 cup sauterne to it. Set aside. Have a sip of wine, then sauté celery and mushrooms in oil. Add green onions, water chestnuts, green pepper, crab, and shrimp. Add the white sauce with wine. This can be refrigerated and baked later if you wish, giving you time to finish your wine. When ready to bake, place the noodles on the bottom of a 2-quart casserole dish and pour cream sauce mixture on top of noodles. Top with almonds and bake at 350° for 30 minutes. Serves 6 to 8.

Scallops Á La Broccoli

This fresh seafood and vegetable dish provides two of the basic four food groups that we need to eat every day for good health. Let's sip on a white table wine such as Chenin Blanc which goes so well with any seafood dish. Be sure and save some for dinner.

66 / Sip and Stir

1 1/2 pounds fresh scallops
1 1/2 cups white table wine
1 pound fresh broccoli
1/2 teaspoon salt
1/2 cup melted butter
1 tablespoon lemon juice

Isn't this good wine! I hope you opened a large bottle. Rinse and drain the scallops and combine with the wine in a sauce pan. Bring to a boil and simmer for 10 minutes. Drain and cut into 1/4-inch slices. Cook fresh broccoli until tender in a minimum amount of water. If not in season, use a frozen package and follow the cooking directions on the box. Drain and arrange the broccoli in the bottom of a low baking dish. Top with the scallop slices and sprinkle with salt. Melt butter and stir in the lemon juice and pour over the scallops and broccoli. Bake at 350° for 10 minutes. Be sure it is served hot. Save the wine in which you cooked the scallops for a chowder. I also save the water in which vegetables are cooked to use for soups; it contains the water-soluble vitamins B and C.

Wine-Poached Salmon with Pretzels

When Dad catches that "big one" try serving it poached in wine with a crushed pretzel topping. The ingredients are for 2 pounds of fish; if the fish is larger, just increase the ingredients accordingly or slice it into steaks and freeze them for another time. Use a rolling pin to crush the pretzels into coarse crumbs. Sip on your favorite white wine as you work.

2 pounds salmon
1 large onion, sliced
2 cups dry white wine
1 teaspoon salt
1/2 cup butter
1 tablespoon grated lemon peel
1 cup crushed pretzels

Line a shallow pan with foil and seal the corners. Place the salmon in the pan and add the onion, wine, and salt. Cover with foil and bake at 350° for 40 minutes. The fish will flake and be a pink color when done. Place salmon on a platter and garnish with parsley and lemon slices. Melt butter, add lemon peel, and pour over the salmon. Sprinkle crushed pretzels over the fish just before serving.

Wine-Topped Ham Rolls

This is an elegant luncheon dish that is easy to prepare. Use any white table wine that you have on hand. My favorite is Chenin Blanc; if you have to buy a bottle, try it. The wine is mild and dry and is excellent for sipping any time.

1 package frozen chopped spinach
1 tablespoon vinegar
1/4 teaspoon nutmeg
5 tablespoons butter
1/4 cup flour
1 cup milk
1 cup white wine

1 cup grated cheddar cheese
12 slices boiled ham

Cook spinach according to package directions. When done drain and season with vinegar, nutmeg, and 2 tablespoons of the butter. Have a sip of Chenin Blanc and make a white sauce. Melt the 3 tablespoons of butter in a saucepan. Stir in the flour and mix until well blended. Gradually add the milk and wine, stirring constantly until it thickens. Stir in the grated cheese. Relax with the rest of your wine before assembling the rolls. Put about 2 tablespoons of spinach on one side of the ham slice and roll toward the center; fasten with a toothpick. Place the rolls about 1/2 inch apart in a greased baking dish. Pour cheese sauce over each ham roll. Bake at 425° for 20 minutes. Serves 6.

Dixie Green Beans

Company is coming—a good excuse for trying this different bean dish. Open a bottle of Chianti and start with a small glass as you cook the beans according to the directions on the package until almost done. When they're in season, I use fresh green beans. Now a little more wine and on to the sauce.

2 packages frozen green beans
3 slices bacon
1 onion, chopped
1/2 cup celery, sliced
2 tablespoons flour
1/4 teaspoon garlic powder

1 cup chicken broth
1/2 cup Chianti wine

Cook bacon until crisp. Remove from the pan and drain on a paper towel. Add onion and celery to the fat and cook until tender. Have a sip. Stir in flour, garlic powder, chicken broth, and Chianti wine and cook until it thickens. Pour over the beans in a casserole and crumble bacon on top. Bake at 350° for 30 minutes. Is there enough wine left for dinner?

Holiday Rice

This is a dressed up version of fried rice. The red and green combination makes it delightful for the holidays. The wine adds a robust flavor.

1 cup uncooked rice
1/2 cup onion, chopped
2 tablespoons butter
1 1/2 cups chicken broth
1/2 cup sauterne wine
1 package frozen spinach
1/4 cup cashew nuts
2 tomatoes

After the first sip, brown the rice and onion in butter. Stir in the chicken broth and wine and simmer for 20 minutes or until the rice is done. Cook and drain the spinach and stir into the rice with the nuts. Slice the tomatoes and arrange on top. Bake at 350° for 20 minutes.

Potatoes on the Rhine

At last, a different way to serve instant potatoes and wait until you taste them! The wine imparts just enough flavor to enhance the rest of the vegetables in this dish. We think you'll like these potatoes well enough to put them on your company list. Rhine wine is a good sipping wine; let's start with a large glass.

1/4 cup butter
1/2 cup chopped celery
1 onion, sliced
1 tomato, diced
1/2 cup sliced olives
2 cups chicken broth
1/2 cup Rhine wine
2 1/2 cups instant potatoes
2 tablespoons chopped parsley
1 teaspoon salt

You won't have much time for sipping once you start this dish. It should be served immediately, so let's have one more sip before we start. We always check the liquid to potato ratio; it varies in different brands. You may need to change the amount of chicken broth for your instant potatoes. Melt the butter in a large skillet and add celery, onion, tomato, and olives; sauté until tender but not brown. Keep heat low. In a saucepan combine chicken broth and wine and bring to a boil. Stir in potatoes, parsley, and salt. Take a quick sip and spoon potatoes into serving dish. Make a hole in the center and fill with the sautéed vegetables.

Stuffed Zucchini

This dish takes a little time but the results are worth your efforts. You will even win over some new zucchini eaters from your anti-squash friends and family members. I like to use fresh vegetables whenever possible and zucchini is often a good buy. Let's sip on Chablis as we prepare this dish.

6 zucchini, trimmed
1/4 cup onion, minced
1/4 cup celery, minced
1/4 cup green pepper, diced small
2 tablespoons butter or margarine
1/2 teaspoon salt
2 eggs, beaten
1/4 cup white wine
1 cup cooked white rice
3/4 cup grated cheddar cheese

Halve zucchini lengthwise; parboil only until tender-crisp; drain and cool slightly. Scoop out pulp and chop into small cubes. Set shells aside. Sauté onion, celery, and green pepper in butter until tender (about 5 minutes). Add salt, zucchini pulp, eggs, white wine, and rice. Arrange shells in a buttered casserole. Stuff shells and bake for 30 minutes at 375°. Sprinkle cheese over top and return to oven for 5 minutes. Serves 6.

4
Red Wines

TOSTADA BEAN DIP
BURGUNDY-BURGER
  SOUP
BURGUNDY-MEATBALL
  SOUP
CRANBERRY-PORT
  SALAD
BERRYPATCH CHICKEN
BROILED WINEBURGERS
BURGUNDY-BEAN STEW
BURGUNDY SPAGHETTI
  SAUCE

GERMAN-STYLE STEW
MEATBALL BRACERS
MEATBALL-CLARET
  CASSEROLE
SUPER SUPPER SURPRISE
VINTAGE CASSEROLE
ITALIAN POTATOES
BAKED APPLES SUPREME
BURGUNDY-CRANBERRY
  CHIFFON PIE
CHRISTMAS
  WINE JELLY

Tostada Bean Dip

Have plenty of corn chips around this dip; it will prove to be a party favorite. The ingredients impart a flavor similar to the popular tostada dish of the West. If avocados are not available, use a tomato instead.

1 can pork and beans
1/2 cup tomato sauce
1/2 cup burgundy wine
1 small onion, chopped
1/2 teaspoon chili powder
1/2 teaspoon Worcestershire sauce
1/2 cup crushed corn chips
1 avocado
1/4 cup grated cheese

Pour a glass of burgundy and get out the blender. Combine all the ingredients except the cheese in the blender, taking time out for a few sips. Blend until smooth (about 30 seconds). This is good served hot or cold and garnished with the grated cheese.

Burgundy-Burger Soup

This is a combination hamburger-vegetable soup that is almost a meal in itself. Since cooking time is about 1 hour pour yourself a large glass of wine.

5 cups water
6 beef bouillon cubes
2 cups tomatoes
1 large onion, diced
1 cup celery, diced
2 carrots, sliced

1/4 teaspoon garlic salt
1/2 teaspoon salt
1 package frozen brussel sprouts
1 teaspoon chili powder
1 cup burgundy wine
1 pound ground beef

Combine water and bouillon cubes in a large pan and simmer until dissolved. Add all ingredients except the ground beef. Let simmer 45 minutes. As you measure the wine, pour yourself another glass. In a skillet, brown the hamburger. Pour off excess fat and add the meat to the soup, cooking 15 minutes more. Garnish with chopped parsley.

Burgundy-Meatball Soup

This is a prize-winning soup that won a $1,000 recipe contest sponsored by the Reginia Winery in California. We have used it many times and it always turns out to be a real man pleaser. Plan a luncheon around it and be sure to have the recipe handy for your friends to copy.

3/4 pound ground beef
1/2 pound ground pork
1 egg
1/4 cup bread crumbs
1/2 teaspoon oregano
1/2 teaspoon salt
6 cups beef stock
1 cup burgundy

1 cup tomato puree
1/2 cup chopped celery
1/2 cup chopped onion
2 teaspoons chili powder

Pour a glass of burgundy and combine meat, egg, bread crumbs, oregano, and salt; shape into walnut-sized meatballs. Combine remaining ingredients and bring to a boil. Add the meatballs and simmer for 45 minutes as you finish your wine. Garnish with chopped fresh parsley.

Cranberry-Port Salad

This molded salad makes a fine addition to a turkey, chicken, or duck dinner. The port adds to the tangy flavor of the salad. Open a large bottle of port so you have enough to serve with dinner when you finish sipping.

3 cups fresh cranberries, chopped
3/4 cup sugar
1 cup water
1 package raspberry flavored gelatin (6-ounce)
1 cup port
3 tablespoons lemon juice
1 cup crushed pineapple
3 apples, diced

Chop cranberries with a food chopper or as I do the easy way in a blender. Stir in sugar and let stand for a few minutes. Boil the water and stir in gelatin until dissolved. Have a little more port and stir in the wine and lemon juice. Chill until almost thick. Fold in pineapple, cranberries, and apples. Pour into a mold and chill until set.

Berrypatch Chicken

This is an oven-baked chicken dish that the entire family will enjoy. Loganberry wine is the base of the sauce so start with a large sipping glass and get busy.

1/4 cup butter
1 chicken fryer, cut in serving pieces
flour for dredging
1 pound pork steak
1 cup loganberry wine
1 cup chicken broth
1/4 cup sugar
1 teaspoon salt
2 tablespoons cornstarch
1/4 cup water
1 cup celery, sliced

Melt the butter in a large frying pan. Dredge the chicken in flour and brown in the hot butter. When browned, place in a large casserole dish. Have a sip of wine before cutting the pork steak into 1-inch cubes. Coat with flour and brown in the same pan. When well-browned, have some more wine and add the pork to the chicken. Pour the wine and chicken broth into the meat drippings. Stir in the sugar and salt. Make a paste with the cornstarch and water and stir into the wine mixture until it is thick.

Add the celery and let it simmer for 5 minutes. Pour over the pork and chicken and let it bake at 350° for 45 minutes.

Broiled Wineburgers

Tired of plain old hamburger? Here is a recipe that will put the American favorite into the regal class. Use burgundy wine and let it blend its flavor in the meat for several hours. This will give you ample sipping opportunity.

2 pounds ground round
3 tablespoons chopped parsley
1/2 cup burgundy wine
1 teaspoon rosemary seasoning powder
1/2 teaspoon salt
2 tablespoons minced onions

Combine all the ingredients in a large bowl and blend well. Put in the refrigerator for at least 4 hours. Before you put the wine away have another glass. It's a reward for picking out such an easy recipe. Just before you are ready to broil the meat, shape it into 6 patties. This will allow 1/3 of a pound per serving. You will have time for sipping while they cook.

Burgundy-Bean Stew

This is a weekday supper dish that combines hamburger and hot dogs and will be a hit with the entire family. The burgundy lends a subtle flavor that blends with the ingredients. Serve it with garlic bread, a green salad, and a bottle of burgundy wine.

1 pound ground beef
1 onion, chopped
1 can tomato soup
1/2 cup burgundy wine
1 can garbanzo beans
1 can red kidney beans
4 hot dogs, sliced

Have a sip of burgundy as you brown the hamburger and onion together. Pour off the fat and combine with the rest of the ingredients in a casserole dish. Bake at 350° for 45 minutes. Serves 6.

Burgundy Spaghetti Sauce

2 tablespoons olive oil
1 medium onion
2 cloves garlic
1 pound ground beef
1 large can tomatoes
1 can tomato paste
1/4 cup burgundy
1 envelope spaghetti seasoning
1/4 teaspoon salt
2 bay leaves
1 can mushrooms

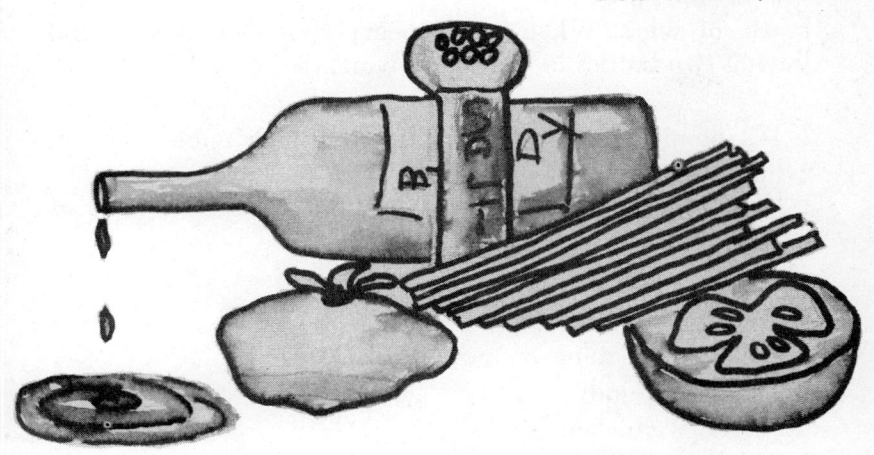

Get out the burgundy and pour a glass for yourself. In a Dutch oven, brown onion and garlic in the olive oil. When these are golden, add the ground beef. Have another sip while the meat browns. Add tomatoes, tomato paste, and burgundy. Mix well and then add seasoning, salt, bay leaves, and mushrooms. Stir this again and let simmer for 3 to 4 hours. Now you are free to take the remainder of the bottle and relax with a good book. Don't forget to take an occasional break from your bottle and book to stir the sauce.

German-Style Stew

This recipe originally came from an Iowa farm. It is a hearty meal in itself. We like it with French bread and a bottle of wine. When you grocery shop, we recommend buying two bottles of burgundy wine.

1 1/2 pounds round steak, cut into 1 inch cubes
2 tablespoons cooking oil
1 large apple, peeled and grated
1 onion, sliced
2 carrots, grated
1/2 cup celery, sliced
1 clove garlic, minced
1/2 cup burgundy
1 1/2 cups chicken broth
2 tablespoons cornstarch
1/4 cup water
4 cups noodles, cooked and drained

If you don't have one, invest in a good corkscrew because the best wines are corked. Makeshift utensils often leave part of the cork in the wine—this is tough and does not enhance most recipes. If there is a man around, let him remove the cork. This will cost you at least one glass of wine before you even start.

Brown the meat in hot oil and add the apple, onion, carrots, celery, and garlic. Stir in wine and chicken broth; cover and let simmer for 2 hours or until the meat is tender. When I stew a chicken, I always save the stock. If you have none, use 1 1/2 cups water with 2 chicken bouillon cubes. Combine cornstarch and 1/4 cup water to make a paste; stir into the stew and cook until thick. Serve over hot noodles.

Meatball Bracers

If it's a hot day make a wine cooler: burgundy wine with soda or 7-Up and ice. This is a meal in a dish, so you'll soon have supper ready.

1 package frozen broccoli
1 pound ground beef
1 tablespoon dried onion
1/4 cup bread crumbs
1 teaspoon salt
1/4 cup catsup
1/2 cup burgundy wine
1 cup tomato sauce
1/4 teaspoon garlic powder

Thaw the broccoli and place in a casserole dish. Make the meatballs by combining the beef, onion, bread crumbs, salt, and catsup. You should have at least 12 meatballs to place on top of the broccoli. After a sip of your cooler, prepare the sauce by simmering the wine, tomato sauce and garlic for 10 minutes. Pour over the meatballs and broccoli. Bake at 375° for 45 minutes. Serves 4. After eating this dish your family will be braced for an evening of fun so be prepared; have another wine cooler!

Meatball-Claret Casserole

Red wine, meatballs, and pasta are combined in this simple supper casserole. It freezes beautifully so make a double batch as you sip on your favorite claret wine.

Sip and Stir

1 package noodles (8 ounces)
1 pound ground beef
1 egg
1/2 cup bread crumbs
1/4 teaspoon garlic powder
1 celery stalk, grated
1/2 teaspoon salt
1/2 cup sliced onion
2 tablespoons salad oil
1 cup sliced mushrooms
1 1/2 cups tomato sauce
1/2 teaspoon oregano
1 cup claret wine
1 cup cottage cheese
2 tablespoons grated Parmesan cheese

As you sip your first glass of wine, cook the noodles according to package directions and drain. Combine ground beef, egg, bread crumbs, garlic powder, celery, and salt, and shape into small meatballs. Brown meatballs and onion in hot oil as you sip on your wine. Add mushrooms, tomato sauce and oregano and simmer for 20 minutes. Stir in wine and pour yourself another glass. In a casserole, layer noodles, cottage cheese, and meatballs twice. Sprinkle with Parmesan cheese. Bake at 375° for 40 minutes.

Super Supper Surprise

Here is a quick dish that the men in your house will ask for again and again. It combines hamburger and beans with a highlight of burgundy wine. Pour a glass and let's get started.

1 pound ground beef
1/4 pound sausage
1 onion, chopped
1 can green beans
1 can kidney beans
1/4 cup brown sugar
1 tablespoon wine vinegar
1 cup tomato sauce
1 teaspoon salt
1/2 cup burgundy wine
2 teaspoons chili powder

Brown the beef, sausage, and onion together in a frying pan. Drain off excess fat. Have a little burgundy and then open the beans. Combine all the ingredients and simmer for 10 minutes. Plenty of sipping time here as you stir occasionally. Pour into a casserole and bake at 350° for 30 minutes and you have dinner practically made. It will go great with garlic bread, a big salad, and the rest of the burgundy.

Vintage Casserole

This hot dish combines sausage and lima beans accented with your favorite red table wine. It makes an easy dinner and calls for a light dessert, maybe just fruit and cheese.

1 package frozen lima beans
1 pound sausage
1 onion, chopped
1/2 cup tomato sauce
1/2 cup red wine
1/2 teaspoon salt
1 teaspoon chili powder
1 cup pitted ripe olives
1 cup grated cheese

Cook lima beans according to the package directions and drain. While the beans are cooking have a sip of your favorite red wine and brown the sausage and onion in a skillet. Pour off fat. Add tomato sauce, red wine, salt, chili powder, and olives. Simmer for 10 minutes as you sip on your wine. Combine with beans in a casserole and top with grated cheese. Bake at 375° for 40 minutes.

Italian Potatoes

We have a friend who comes over for dinner frequently and he is strictly a meat and potato man, turning down all other vegetables. One night I had an Italian eggplant casserole and we passed the dish to him and said, "try some Italian potatoes." Three helpings later we finally confessed, but he still calls them "Italian potatoes" and we do too. Sip on Chianti as you prepare this surprise for your family and friends.

1 eggplant, peeled and sliced in 1/2-inch slices
1 egg, beaten

1 cup cornflake crumbs
3/4 cup salad oil
salt to taste
1 cup grated Mozzarella cheese
1/2 cup Chianti
1 can tomato sauce (8 ounces)

Dip eggplant slices into egg and then roll in cornflake crumbs. Fry in oil until brown and tender. Remove and drain on absorbent paper. Salt slices and arrange in a casserole in alternate layers of cheese. Add Chianti to tomato sauce and pour over eggplant mixture. Bake at 375° for 20 minutes.

Baked Apples Supreme

This is a dish with multi-uses. It can be served as a fruit for breakfast, hot or cold. I often use it as a dessert, stuffing the apples with a mixture of grated cheddar cheese, nuts, and cream cheese and topped with whipped cream. I've also used the wine-cooked apples for a salad by stuffing them with a mixture of cream cheese, celery, nuts, and mayonnaise. Have some wine and dream up your own version.

4 large cooking apples
1 cup red wine
1 cup sugar
1 teaspoon cinnamon
3 cloves
1/4 teaspoon salt
red food coloring

Peel and remove the core from the apples. Place in a baking dish. Have a sip of wine and combine the rest of the ingredients in a sauce pan. Add a few drops of red food coloring and bring to a boil. Simmer for 5 minutes. Pour the syrup mixture over the apples and bake at 350° for 40 minutes. Baste several times with the syrup. Serve hot with the sauce or chill and serve with whipped cream.

Burgundy-Cranberry Chiffon Pie

This is my favorite holiday pie for both Thanksgiving and Christmas. It is light, pretty, and tastes good after a big meal. However, I usually wait and serve it at least an hour after dinner when everyone can enjoy it more. I make it the night before the big day when I need to be fortified with a little sipping; that means having a large bottle of burgundy on hand.

1/2 cup sugar
1/4 cup flour
1 envelope gelatin
1 cup cranberry juice
1 cup burgundy wine
3 egg whites
1/3 cup sugar
1/2 cup cream, whipped
1 graham cracker crust

Combine sugar, flour, gelatin, juice, and wine. Mix well and cook over medium heat, stirring until thick. Chill until mixture mounds when spooned. This gives you a good sipping break. Beat egg whites and add 1/3 cup sugar. Fold into the cranberry mixture. Fold in the whipped cream. Pour into prepared pie shell. Garnish with green grapes and additional whipped cream. Chill until set and have a sip.

Christmas Wine Jelly

Start collecting attractive jars and glasses long before Christmas because you will want to give friends a sample of this jelly for the holidays. I usually make my Christmas jelly right after Thanksgiving so that it will have time to age. I have used a variety of fruit wines which are all excellent for sipping anytime. Cherry, blueberry, loganberry, and raspberry wines all make excellent jellies.

2 cups cranberry juice
6 cups sugar
1 bottle Certo
2 cups wine

This jelly is easy to make and goes very fast. Pour some wine and begin sipping as you sterilize your jars and glasses. Measure all the ingredients and have them ready to add. Combine the cranberry juice and sugar in a large heavy kettle. Put on high heat and bring to a rolling boil. Boil for 1 minute. Add the Certo and boil again for 1 minute. Stir in the wine, but do not boil again. Let it cool for 5 minutes while you do some more sipping. Skim the top of the jelly with a metal spoon and pour the clear jelly into jars. Seal with paraffin. The next time you cook cornish game hens try basting them with this jelly.

5
Fruit Wines

ORANGE-GLAZED
  HOT DOGS
HANGOVER AMBROSIA
APPLE-CORN
  RELISH SALAD
WINE-O SALAD
BARBECUED SPARERIBS
DIXIE HAM CASSEROLE
TUNA PIE
BAKED VEGETABLE
  DISH
EGGPLANT BOATS
APPLE WINE MUFFINS
ORANGE-APRICOT
  SECRET BREAD

PUMPKIN-NUT BREAD
APPLE WINE CAKE
APRICOT ROYAL
BERRY DELIGHT
FRUIT AND DUMPLINGS
GRANDMA'S SECRET
  CAKE
LEMON BISQUE FLIP
STEAMED APRICOT
  BREAD PUDDING
STRAWBERRY-
  LEMONADE PIE
STRAWBERRY
  ROYALE CAKE
YUMMIE YAMMIES
WINE SAUCE

Orange-Glazed Hot Dogs

Having a party? Here is an inexpensive and easy way to prepare an appetizer that will disappear almost as soon as you put it out. Use sliced hot dogs or, if you want to be fancier, use the small canned cocktail frankfurters. On occasions, I have used cubes of bologna and Spam with the same sauce.

2 cups orange juice
2/3 cup honey
2 tablespoons orange peel
1 cup Madeira wine
1/2 teaspoon oregano
1 teaspoon Grand Marnier
1/4 cup prepared mustard
2 tablespoons cornstarch
2 pounds wieners
2 oranges, peeled and sectioned

Heat all ingredients except wieners and oranges over low heat until it thickens slightly. Stir and sip on your wine frequently. Add the wieners and orange sections until they are glazed. Serve hot in a chafing dish with toothpicks. When adding cornstarch to thicken a liquid, we usually make a paste first by combining the cornstarch with 1/4 cup of liquid; we used part of the orange juice. This insures a smooth sauce with no lumps.

Hangover Ambrosia

This is an extra special fresh fruit salad for a brunch or dessert. The fresh fruit is combined with blackberry wine gelatin cubes. This takes at least two glasses of blackberry wine for drinking—one while you make the gelatin, and one several hours later when you prepare the fruits.

1 package raspberry flavored gelatin (3 ounces)
3/4 cup boiling water
3/4 cup blackberry wine
4 oranges
2 grapefruits
2 bananas
1 box strawberries
1 fresh pineapple

Start with a large glass of blackberry wine because it tastes good. Pour the boiling water over the gelatin and stir until it dissolves. Stir in the wine. Pour into a rectangular cake pan and chill until set. Cut into one-inch cubes.

Peel and section oranges and grapefruit, slice bananas,

and clean and hull strawberries. Trim pineapple and cut into chunks. Combine fruits with wine cubes in a bowl and mix well. If you want a dressing, use pineapple yogurt. Now finish your wine.

Apple-Corn Relish Salad

This is a salad in which you use fresh unpeeled apples. We like pippins best but any type will do. If you have a real apple peel hater in the family, like my father, you may have to peel the apples first. It is easy to prepare and should be chilled at least 12 hours before serving. It will keep up to a week in the refrigerator.

2 tablespoons cornstarch
1/2 cup apple wine
2 cups whole kernel corn
1/3 cup sugar
1/3 cup vinegar
1 teaspoon turmeric
1/4 cup chopped onion
1/4 teaspoon celery seed
2 tablespoons chopped pimento
2 apples, chopped

I begin with a large glass of apple wine before I assemble all the ingredients. After a sip, make a paste of the cornstarch and apple wine and stir into the rest of the ingredients in a saucepan. Cook and stir until relish thickens and boils. Let it simmer for about 5 minutes. Apples will still be crisp. Refrigerate until well chilled. Serve on lettuce as a salad or as a relish accompaniment with most meats.

Wine-O Salad

If you haven't had the pleasure of trying apricot wine, then you are in for a real treat. Open a bottle and pour a little into a liqueur glass. It is so good when chilled.

1 can crushed pineapple, drained (29 ounces)
1 can apricots, drained and finely cut (29 ounces)
1 package orange or orange-pineapple flavored gelatin (6 ounces)
3 1/2 cups water
1/2 cup apricot wine
1 3/4 cups miniature marshmallows

Drain the fruits and reserve the juice for the topping. Dissolve the gelatin in 2 cups boiling water. Then stir in 1 1/2 cups cold water and the wine. Have another sip. Mix the apricots, pineapple, and gelatin together. Pour into a 11 x 7 x 2" dish. Sprinkle the marshmallows over the top. Chill until firm. How about another glass of wine?

Fruit Topping:

1/2 cup sugar
3 tablespoons flour
1 egg, slightly beaten
1 cup combined apricot and pineapple juice
1 package cream cheese (8 ounces)
grated cheese or chopped nuts

Combine sugar and flour; blend in beaten egg. Gradually stir in juice until smooth. Cook over low heat, stirring constantly until thick. Remove from heat and allow to cool. When cool, beat in cream cheese and spread over the gelatin layer. Sprinkle with grated cheese or chopped nuts.

Barbecued Spareribs

This will be a favorite your family will ask for again and again. Start by pouring yourself a glass of honey wine.

2 onions, finely chopped
1 clove garlic, minced
2 tablespoons oil
1 can tomato paste (6 ounces)
1/2 cup catsup
1/4 cup vinegar
1 teaspoon salt
1/2 teaspoon pepper
1 teaspoon paprika
1 teaspoon dry mustard
1 tablespoon brown sugar
1/3 cup honey wine
1/2 cup beef stock
1 tablespoon Worcestershire sauce
4 pounds spareribs

Lightly brown onions and garlic in oil. Combine tomato paste, catsup, vinegar, salt, pepper, paprika, mustard, brown sugar, wine, beef stock, and Worcestershire sauce. Bring to a boil and simmer 15 minutes. This gives you a chance to sip on that delightful honey wine.

Place ribs in a roasting pan with fat side up. Pour sauce over ribs, cover and bake 1 1/2 hours at 350°. Uncover and bake 1/2 hour more to brown. Serves 6.

Dixie Ham Casserole

This is a great dish for using leftover ham. It goes together very quickly so sit down and have a glass of sherry as you read over the recipe.

1/4 pound fresh mushrooms
1 cup sliced celery
1/4 cup butter
1/4 cup flour
2 cups milk
1/2 cup sherry

3 cups hominy
2 cups chopped cooked ham
1/2 cup grated cheddar cheese
1 teaspoon Worcestershire sauce
salt and pepper to taste

Rinse fresh mushrooms in cold water and slice (unless the mushrooms are very small). You may want to leave a few whole. Slice celery diagonally and mix with the mushrooms. Sauté both in melted butter for 5 minutes. Blend in flour and add the milk and sherry slowly. Time to sip and stir until the mixture thickens. You may need to pour yourself another glass of sherry at this point. Add hominy, ham, cheese, Worcestershire sauce, salt, and pepper. Pour into a greased 2-quart casserole and bake at 350° for 40 minutes.

Tuna Pie

More tuna is eaten than any other fish in this country. It's popular with both the young and old. This biscuit-topped casserole will prove a hit with the entire family and you'll get to sip a little Madeira wine as you work in the kitchen.

1 onion, chopped
1/4 cup butter
1/4 cup flour
1/2 teaspoon salt
1 cup water
1/2 cup Madeira wine

1/2 cup milk
2 chicken bouillon cubes
1 can tuna (6 1/2 ounces)
1 cup celery, sliced
3 hard-cooked eggs, sliced
1 can refrigerated biscuits
1/4 cup Parmesan cheese

Sauté onion in melted butter until tender. Add the flour and salt, stirring until smooth. Combine water, wine, milk, and bouillon cubes and add to the onion mixture. Have some wine and sip and stir until the sauce thickens and boils. Add the tuna, celery, and eggs and let simmer 10 minutes. Pour into a baking dish. Arrange biscuits on top in a circle and sprinkle with cheese. Bake at 400° until biscuits are done.

Baked Vegetable Dish

This colorful vegetable casserole will be a welcome addition to any meal. We like to bake it with a roast or with a meat loaf and get double use from our oven as we sip sherry.

1/4 cup chopped onion
1/2 cup sliced celery
2 tablespoons butter
2 cups cream style corn
2 tomatoes, diced
1 teaspoon salt
2 eggs

1 cup garlic flavored croutons
2 tablespoons sherry

Sauté onion and celery in butter until tender. Have a sip of sherry and add corn, tomatoes, and salt. Beat eggs; stir into the corn mixture and add croutons. Pour into a greased casserole dish. I hope you have saved enough sherry to stir into the casserole. Bake at 325° for 1 hour. Garnish with parsley and fresh tomato slices.

Eggplant Boats

You don't know how good eggplant is until you try it! Most of the family won't even know it's eggplant unless you tell them. Serve it sliced in half with the delicious filling on top and watch it disappear just as your sherry does as you "sip and stir."

1 large eggplant
1/2 pound sausage
1/2 cup chopped onion
1/2 cup chopped celery
1/4 cup chopped parsley
1/4 teaspoon paprika
1/4 teaspoon thyme
2 tomatoes, peeled and diced
1 cup cracker crumbs
1/2 cup sherry

Cut eggplant in half lengthwise. Scoop out the pulp and chop it. Leave shell 1/4 inch thick. Time for a sip. Heat and stir sausage in a skillet. Drain off excess fat. Sauté onion, celery, parsley, and eggplant pulp with sausage. Add seasonings, tomatoes, and crumbs. Moisten dressing with sherry as you have a sip. Fill eggplant shells with stuffing. Bake in a greased pan at 375° for 30 minutes or until shell is tender.

Apple Wine Muffins

This is a hot bread that will become a family favorite once you've tried it. It's a real treat for Sunday breakfast or a holiday brunch.

2 cups biscuit mix
1/4 cup sugar
1 teaspoon cinnamon
1/2 cup applesauce

1/4 cup apple wine
1 egg
2 tablespoons salad oil
1/2 cup chopped pecans

Pour a small glass of apple wine and check your ingredients. This goes together very fast. Combine the biscuit mix, sugar, and cinnamon in a bowl and set aside. Have a sip and combine the rest of the ingredients and mix well. Add to the dry ingredients and do not over mix. Stir in chopped pecans. Fill greased muffin tins 1/2 full. Bake at 400° for 15 minutes or until done. Makes 10 muffins.

Orange-Apricot Secret Bread

Are you a lover of holiday breads but in the mood for something different? Here's a quick bread with a secret in its preparation. Let's sip on a glass of apricot wine as we try to discover the secret.

1 cup dried apricots
1 cup sugar
4 teaspoons butter or margarine
1 egg, beaten
3/4 cup orange juice
1/4 cup apricot wine
2 cups flour
2 teaspoons baking powder
1/4 teaspoon soda
1 teaspoon salt
1 cup chopped pecans

Cut apricots in small pieces and soak in warm water for 1/2 hour. Drain and set aside. Combine sugar, butter, egg, orange juice, and wine. Have a sip and mix well. Sift flour, baking powder, soda, and salt; add to sugar mixture. Fold in apricots and pecans. Pour into a greased and floured loaf pan and let stand 20 minutes. Bake at 325° for 1 hour. (The secret is in the standing time.)

Pumpkin-Nut Bread

This is a moist nut bread that is a welcome addition at any breakfast. It keeps well and is a wonderful bread to have on hand during the holidays to serve with coffee, eggnog, or whatever you are serving to those who drop by for a visit. We like to bake it after dinner when someone else is doing the dishes. I allow myself a large sipping glass of sherry.

1 1/2 cups sugar
2 eggs
1/2 cup oil
1/3 cup sherry
1 cup pumpkin
1 3/4 cups sifted flour
1 teaspoon baking soda
3/4 teaspoon salt
1/2 teaspoon nutmeg
1/2 teaspoon cinnamon
1 cup chopped walnuts

After relaxing a minute with your sherry you will find

that this is a quick bread to make. Combine the following in a large bowl: sugar, eggs, oil, sherry, and pumpkin. Beat with an electric mixer for 2 minutes. Have some sherry and stir in the dry ingredients, beating for 2 more minutes. Stir in the nuts. Pour the batter into 2 greased loaf pans. Bake at 350° for 1 hour or until done. Test with a toothpick—it should come out clean.

Apple Wine Cake

This is a good cake to bake in the winter. The delicious smell will attract people to the kitchen, so open a large bottle of apple wine which will help to warm every one. This is a quick and easy cake to prepare and will keep because it is very moist. But it tastes so good, it doesn't last long!

1/2 cup salad oil
1 egg
1 1/2 cups applesauce
1 cup sugar
1/4 cup apple wine
2 cups cake flour
3 tablespoons cocoa
1/4 teaspoon salt
1/2 teaspoon nutmeg
1/2 teaspoon cinnamon
1 1/2 teaspoons baking powder
2 teaspoons soda

Now that you've had your first sip of apple wine let's get started. In a large bowl combine the oil, egg, applesauce, sugar, and apple wine. Use your electric mixer for about 1 minute. Have a sip while you are doing this. Add the rest of the ingredients to the mixture and beat for about 2 minutes. Pour into 2 greased 8-inch cake pans and bake at 375° for 25 minutes.

Apricot Royal

This is a wine fruit dish that you might use for a brunch

or a dessert. It is simple to prepare and keeps well when refrigerated.

2 cups dried apricots
1 cup apricot wine
2 tablespoons slivered orange peel
1 teaspoon lemon juice
1 cup water
1/2 cup white raisins
1/2 cup brown sugar
1/4 teaspoon ginger

Let's start with a sip of apricot wine as you get out your cutting board to sliver the orange peel. Combine apricots, wine, orange peel, and lemon juice, bringing to a boil in a saucepan. Simmer for 30 minutes. The apricots should be tender. Add the rest of the ingredients and simmer for 5 more minutes. Serve cold with the syrup and garnish with almond slices.

Berry Delight

Looking for something different for dessert tonight? Here it is—a rich pudding made with blackberry wine. Make it anytime the day before you want to serve it.

1 package frozen raspberries, thawed
3/4 cup sugar
1 tablespoon lemon juice
1 cup blackberry wine
1/4 cup tapioca, quick cooking
1/2 cup whipping cream

104 / Sip and Stir

1/2 cup vanilla wafer cookie crumbs

I start the dessert with a large glass of blackberry wine because it's one of my favorite sipping wines. It is excellent in coolers, too. In a saucepan combine raspberries, sugar, and lemon juice. Simmer for 10 minutes. Stir in blackberry wine and tapioca until the mixture thickens. Pour into dessert glasses and chill. Just before serving top with whipped cream and sprinkle with crushed vanilla wafers.

Fruit and Dumplings

We have made this dessert with apricots but you can use any fresh fruit that you have at home or, if you are in a real hurry, use a canned fruit as your base and reduce sugar to 1/2 cup. Pour a glass of apricot wine and prepare the fruit.

3 1/2 cups apricot halves
1/2 cup apricot wine
1 cup sugar
1/2 teaspoon nutmeg
1/4 teaspoon salt

Dumplings:

2 eggs, beaten
1 1/2 cups cottage cheese
1 teaspoon cinnamon
1/2 teaspoon salt
2 tablespoons shortening
1 1/2 cups sifted flour

Combine apricot halves and wine in a saucepan and bring to a boil. Stir in sugar, nutmeg and salt and cook and stir until the sugar dissolves. Pour into a shallow baking dish. Have a sip of wine and make your dumplings. Mix the eggs, cottage cheese, cinnamon, and salt. Cut the shortening into the flour with a pastry blender and add to the cottage cheese mixture. Drop by tablespoons onto the prepared fruit. Bake at 400° for 35 minutes. The dumplings should be a pale golden-brown.

Grandma's Secret Cake

What is grandma's secret? A rich, moist cake filled with vitamins and carrots to serve her family when they visit! Grandma also enjoys sipping a little sherry as she bakes this cake.

4 eggs
1 1/2 cups salad oil
2 cups flour
2 cups sugar
2 teaspoons baking powder
2 teaspoons soda
2 teaspoons cinnamon
1 1/2 cups chopped nuts
3 cups finely grated carrots
2 tablespoons cream sherry

Beat eggs and add oil. Sift all dry ingredients and add to eggs and oil. Add nuts, grated carrots, and sherry. Bake in 3 layers at 350° for 45 minutes.

106 / Sip and Stir

Icing:

1 package powdered sugar
1/4 cup butter or margarine
1 teaspoon vanilla
1 package cream cheese (8 ounces)

Beat ingredients until creamy and frost cake—watch the carrot-haters stand in line!

Lemon Bisque Flip

This is a light, airy dessert that combines apple wine and lemon flavor. I like to make it in a loaf pan because it is easy to slice and serve, but you can use any type of dish.

1 1/2 cups crushed graham crackers
2 tablespoons melted butter
1 box lemon flavored gelatin (3 ounces)
1 cup hot water
1/2 cup apple wine
1/2 cup lemon juice
1/2 cup sugar
1 cup whipping cream

Have some apple wine and crush the graham crackers with a rolling pin mixing with the melted butter. Pat half of the crumb mixture into the bottom of a loaf pan. Dissolve the gelatin in hot water. Stir in apple wine, lemon juice, and sugar. Stir until sugar dissolves. Chill until it starts to thicken but is not set. This will give you time to finish your wine and pour another glass. Whip cream until stiff. Beat the gelatin mixture and fold in the whipped cream. Spoon into the loaf pan on top of the crumbs. Sprinkle the remaining crumbs on top. Chill several hours. Garnish with whipped cream and strawberries.

Steamed Apricot Bread Pudding

Here is a modern version of bread pudding. The apricot wine penetrates the pudding as it steams, producing a unique flavor. Serve it in the summer and garnish it with whipped cream and fresh apricots. Now let's open that bottle of apricot wine.

3 tablespoons butter
1/3 cup sugar

108 / Sip and Stir

1 egg
1/4 cup chopped apricots
1/4 cup apricot wine
1/2 cup chopped dates
1/2 cup raisins
1/2 cup chopped walnuts
1/4 cup flour
3/4 cup milk
2 cups dry bread cubes
1/2 teaspoon salt
1 teaspoon baking powder

Mix butter, sugar, and egg together until smooth. Have a sip of your apricot wine. Soak apricots in apricot wine. Combine dates, raisins, and walnuts and mix with the flour. Stir into the egg mixture. Add milk, bread cubes, salt, and baking powder and mix well. Stir in apricot mixture. Pour batter into 1 1/2-quart mold until about 3/4 full. Cover mold with lid or foil and place on rack in a large kettle with boiling water resting halfway up to the mold. Steam for 1 1/2 hours, adding more water if needed. You have plenty of time for sipping.

Strawberry-Lemonade Pie

It can be strawberry season all year long with this pie. The only fresh strawberries that you need are for garnishing. Your fruit flavor comes from the wine and yogurt. You will like sipping on strawberry wine as you make this pie.

1 tablespoon gelatin
1/2 cup sugar
1/4 teaspoon salt
4 eggs, separated
1/4 cup strawberry wine
1/2 cup lemon juice
1/2 teaspoon cream of tartar
1/3 cup sugar
1 cup strawberry yogurt
9-inch baked pie shell

Mix gelatin, 1/2 cup of sugar and salt together in a saucepan. Beat the egg yolks, strawberry wine, and lemon juice together and add to the gelatin mixture. Place over low heat and stir until the sugar dissolves. Pour into a bowl and chill until it is slightly thickened. This will give you time to enjoy a glass of strawberry wine. When the gelatin mixture starts to thicken, beat the egg whites until foamy and beat in the cream of tartar and sugar, adding a little at a time. Beat until stiff. Fold the gelatin mixture and the yogurt into the egg whites. Pour into pie shell and chill until firm. Garnish with whipped cream and fresh strawberries.

Strawberry Royale Cake

Strawberry wine is quite good to sip. Pour a glass and sip on it while we make a simple white cake very tasty.

1 white cake mix
1 cup strawberry wine

110 / Sip and Stir

1 box frozen strawberries, partly thawed
1 large carton prepared whipped topping

Bake cake in a 13 x 9 x 2" pan according to package directions. Immediately after taking the cake from the oven, punch full of holes and pour strawberry wine over the cake. Refill your glass at the same time. Set cake aside to cool.

At the time of serving, frost cake with a box of frozen strawberries mixed in a carton of whipped topping.

Yummie Yammies

It's cookie baking time again. This cake-like cookie disappears like magic, so you'd better make a double batch!

3/4 cup sugar
3/4 cup shortening
1 egg
1 cup cooked mashed sweet potatoes
2 teaspoons baking powder
2 cups sifted flour
3 tablespoons sherry
1/2 cup chopped walnuts

Combine sugar and shortening and mix until smooth. Pour a glass of sherry for sipping. Stir in egg and mashed sweet potatoes—I used canned ones unless I have some left over from dinner. Stir them into the batter and have a little sherry. Stir in the dry ingredients alternately with the sherry. Mix well and stir in the nuts. Drop by teaspoon onto a greased cookie sheet. Bake at 400° for 12 to 15 minutes.

Orange Icing:
Don't drink all the sherry—save at least a few drops for the icing:

1 tablespoon orange juice
2 tablespoons butter
1 1/2 cups powdered sugar

Mix the butter and part of the sugar together until smooth. Stir in orange juice, a few drops of sherry, and the rest of the sugar. If it is too dry, add a little more sherry and stir until smooth.

Wine Sauce

This is a sauce that will glorify the simplest pudding. It can be served hot or cold. We like it served hot over our carrot pudding. We will be sipping Madeira wine.

3/4 cup sugar
2 teaspoons cornstarch
3/4 cup Madeira wine
1/4 cup water
1/2 teaspoon lemon juice
1/2 teaspoon grated lemon rind
1/4 teaspoon nutmeg
2 eggs, well beaten

Combine sugar and cornstarch in the top of a double boiler over boiling water. Slowly add wine, water, lemon juice, rind and nutmeg. Have your wine close as we will sip and stir constantly for the next 5 minutes. Pour the mixture over well-beaten eggs; return to the top of the double boiler and cook until the sauce will coat a spoon.

6
Rum

HAM SLICES WITH
   RUM SAUCE
MAI TAI STEAK
HONEY-RUM
   ACORN SQUASH
CALYPSO BREAD
ISLAND MUFFINS
AUNT ANNIE'S
   RICE PUDDING
BILL'S FROZEN
   BANANAS
CARROT PUDDING

CARIBBEAN RUM CAKE
HOT PINEAPPLE
   SHORTCAKE
MACAROON ISLAND
   DELIGHT
PEACH AND RUM
   SHORTCAKE NESTS
RUM DUMS
RUM SNOWBALLS
SECOND PIECE
SOUR CREAM RUM CAKE
SUGAR DADDY CAKE
TRINIDAD NUT LOAVES

Ham Slices with Rum Sauce

This is a rum-braced fruit sauce to top baked ham or

ham slices. It is easy to do and really dresses up a ham. Let's use the blender and make a frozen daiquiri to sip.

1/2 cup apple juice
1/2 cup orange juice
1/4 cup rum
1/2 cup pineapple juice
2 tablespoons cornstarch
1 tablespoon vinegar
1/2 cup raisins
1 teaspoon Worcestershire sauce
1/2 cup brown sugar
1 teaspoon prepared mustard

Combine all the ingredients in a saucepan. Cook and stir over medium heat until thick and clear. Baste ham slices with the sauce during the last 30 minutes of cooking. This gives you time for another daiquiri. Serve the rest of the sauce on the ham.

Mai Tai Steak

If you have ever been to Hawaii, you become a quick fan of the Mai Tai which is a popular drink in the islands. We have combined the fruit flavor and rum in this unusual steak dish. Mix a Mai Tai and prepare the marinade sauce.

1 envelope instant meat marinade
1 cup pineapple juice
1/2 cup orange juice
1 tablespoon lemon juice

1/4 cup rum
1/2 teaspoon ginger
2 pounds flank steak
2 tablespoons cornstarch
1/4 cup water

Isn't that Mai Tai good? Combine the instant marinade, fruit juices, rum, and ginger. Place the steak in the marinade sauce for one hour. Turn frequently as you sip on your Mai Tai. Remove steak and drain marinade into a saucepan. Combine cornstarch and water to make a smooth paste and pour into the sauce. Cook and stir until sauce thickens and boils; simmer for 5 minutes. Broil the steak for about 5 minutes on each side or until done. Carve meat into thin diagonal slices and top with sauce. Garnish with pineapple spears.

Honey-Rum Acorn Squash

We think you will like this rum flavored squash. We have allowed one half squash per serving; you may want to cut down, depending on your menu. Squash is a high carbohydrate vegetable and should not be served with rice or potatoes. Mix a rum and collins and start dinner.

3 medium-sized acorn squash
1/4 cup butter
1/2 teaspoon salt
1/4 teaspoon ginger
1/4 cup honey
2 tablespoons rum
1 tablespoon sesame seeds

Just getting to sip on a rum and collins makes preparing this vegetable worthwhile. Scrub the squash, cut in half lengthwise, and clean. Arrange in a shallow baking dish with the cut side down and pour about 1 inch of water into the pan. Bake at 375° for 30 minutes. Have a sip of your drink and combine the remaining ingredients in a saucepan and cook and stir until the butter melts. After 30 minutes remove squash from the oven and pour off any remaining water; turn squash so the cut side is up. Pour sauce into the hole and bake 20 minutes more. Sip and baste several times. Serves 6.

Calypso Bread

You'll feel like singing once you've tasted this rum-laced banana bread. It will make coffee break a real treat when friends drop in for a short visit. It keeps well and the flavor improves with age. Let's sip on Planters Punch while we work in the kitchen.

2/3 cup sugar
1/3 cup shortening
1 egg
2 tablespoons rum
1 3/4 cups sifted flour
2 teaspoons baking powder
1/4 teaspoon baking soda
1/2 teaspoon salt
1 cup mashed bananas (2 or 3)

Cream sugar and shortening until smooth. Have a sip of punch and stir in egg and rum. Add the dry ingredients and bananas a little at a time and mix well. Pour into a greased loaf pan and bake at 350° for 50 minutes or until done.

Island Muffins

This hot bread will highlight a brunch, luncheon or Hawaiian supper. There is just enough rum in it to give a faint "I'm not sure what it is" flavor. Better make a double batch, because almost everyone will ask for seconds. If you do have a few left, they are great from the freezer and warmed up before serving. If I am having a luau, I like to do my sipping on a Mai Tai.

2 cups prepared biscuit mix
2 tablespoons sugar
1/4 cup coconut

1/2 teaspoon baking soda
2 tablespoons oil
1 egg, beaten
1 cup pineapple yogurt
1 tablespoon rum

The Mai Tai almost puts me out of a cooking mood so hurry and combine the biscuit mix, sugar, coconut, and baking soda. Have a sip and add the rest of the ingredients. Stir until all the dry ingredients are moistened. Do not over beat. Fill greased muffin tins until 2/3 full. Bake at 400° for 15 minutes or until done. This will give you time to finish your Mai Tai.

Aunt Annie's Rice Pudding

This is an old-fashioned rice pudding that will taste just as good today and bring back some fond memories. Aunt Annie sipped on hot buttered rum—let's give it a try!

2 1/2 cups milk
1/2 cup rice
1/2 teaspoon salt
1 cup raisins
1/2 cup sugar
2 tablespoons flour
1 tablespoon butter
1/4 cup sliced almonds
1 egg
2 tablespoons rum

This hot buttered rum is good, but you have to sip slowly. Combine the milk, rice, and salt and bring to a boil. Add the raisins, sugar, flour, butter, and almonds and mix well. Remove from the heat. Beat the egg and rum together and stir into the mixture. Pour into a greased casserole and bake at 400° for 40 minutes. Aunt Annie ate her pudding with fresh cream, but we like milk and sugar on ours.

Bill's Frozen Bananas

We had a friend visiting from Boston who was fascinated by the chocolate-covered frozen bananas that are sold at the beaches in California. We experimented and came up with this recipe for him to try on his friends in Boston. He liked sipping on rum and Coke, maybe you will, too.

6 ripe bananas
1 cup semi-sweet chocolate chips
2 tablespoons butter
1 tablespoon rum
1 cup finely chopped nuts

We found it easier to work with half a banana. Have a sip and peel and cut bananas in half. Insert a wooden stick in the end of each. Place in a shallow pan and freeze. It will take about 3 hours. Melt butter with the chocolate chips over hot water and stir in the rum. Dip frozen bananas into the mixture and roll in the nuts. Chocolate will harden quickly. Wrap bananas and store in freezer or eat immediately with Bill.

Carrot Pudding

This is a dessert to cook on a cold winter day as you will need the oven on for several hours. It is filled with fruits and vegetables that are so important to our daily health. Enjoy a hot rum toddy as you work in the kitchen.

1 cup apples
1 cup potatoes + 1 teaspoon soda
1 cup carrots
1 cup bread crumbs
1 cup raisins
1 cup nuts
1 cup sifted flour
2 tablespoons shortening
1/2 teaspoon salt
1 cup currants

1 cup sugar
3 eggs in 1 cup (finish filling cup with milk)
1/4 cup rum
1 teaspoon each, lemon rind, allspice, cinnamon, and nutmeg

Grind apples, potatoes, carrots, and bread crumbs together. Be sure to sprinkle the potatoes with the soda to help them retain their color. Mix in all other ingredients and put in a well-greased 4-quart mold or several cans. Cover mold with a tight lid or foil and place on a rack in a large kettle with boiling water resting halfway up to the mold. Add water if needed. Keep the water boiling for 4 hours.

Caribbean Rum Cake

Do you want something different to serve to your bridge group or that will stand out at a potluck dinner? Then try this spicy rum cake. I like it because the frosting is different and easy to do.

1/2 cup shortening
1 1/3 cups sugar
2 eggs
1/4 cup rum
1 cup mashed ripe bananas (3 bananas)
2 cups sifted flour
1 1/2 teaspoons baking powder
1 teaspoon baking soda
1 teaspoon salt

122 / Sip and Stir

1/2 teaspoon nutmeg
1/2 cup walnuts, chopped

Topping:
1 cup sour cream
1/3 cup brown sugar
1/4 cup coconut

Let's sip on a rum and Coke as we work. Cream the sugar and shortening together until smooth. Add eggs and mix well. Have a sip and stir in the rum and mashed bananas. If you are using an electric mixer, beat it for about 2 minutes. Add dry ingredients and beat for 2 more minutes. Stir in the nuts and have a little more rum and Coke. Spread the batter into a greased 9 x 9 x 2" pan. Bake at 350° for 35 minutes. Finish your drink and mix the sour cream and brown sugar together. Spread over warm cake and sprinkle with coconut; bake 8 minutes longer. Cool and cut.

Hot Pineapple Shortcake

This is a filling dessert that tastes great after a light supper. Sometimes we eat early on Sunday afternoon and have our dessert later in the evening. This is one of those dishes that you want to be hungry enough to really enjoy. Dad will like the rum flavor. Let's sip on a Rum Collins as we bake the cake.

1/2 cup sugar
1/4 cup shortening

1 egg
1 teaspoon vanilla
1 cup sifted cake flour
1/4 teaspoon salt
1 1/4 teaspoons baking powder
1/4 cup milk plus 2 tablespoons

Topping:
1 cup pineapple juice
1 tablespoon cornstarch
3/4 cup sugar
1/4 cup rum
1 can pineapple chunks or
    1 1/2 cups of fresh pineapple pieces

    Mix sugar and shortening together; add the egg and mix well. Stir in the vanilla; measure the dry ingredients and add alternately with the milk. Mix well. Pour into a greased 8-inch square pan. Bake at 375° for 25 minutes as you finish sipping your Rum Collins. Combine the pineapple juice, cornstarch, and sugar in a saucepan. Cook and stir until the sugar dissolves and the mixture thickens. Stir in the rum and pineapple chunks. Cut the warm cake into squares. While still warm, poke a hole in the top and fill with pineapple chunks and glaze. Garnish with whipped cream and fresh strawberries.

Macaroon Island Delight

    This Hawaiian-inspired dessert is easier to make than you might think at first glance and the results are well worth your efforts. It calls for Mai Tai sipping to put you in a real island mood.

1 dozen macaroon cookies
1/4 cup rum
1/2 cup chopped nuts
2 tablespoons gelatin
1 cup water
2 cups scalded milk
4 eggs, separated
1 cup sugar
1 cup coconut
1 tablespoon rum

Put down your Mai Tai and get out a spring pan. Line the bottom of the pan with the macaroon cookies. Pour 1/4 cup of rum over the cookies and sprinkle with the nuts. Have a sip and soak the gelatin in cold water. Combine the milk, egg yolks, and sugar and cook and stir until it thickens. Add the gelatin mixture and stir until it dissolves. Let it cool in the refrigerator until it starts to thicken and stir in the coconut. Beat egg whites until stiff and fold into the gelatin mixture. Stir in 1 tablespoon of rum and spoon the mixture over the rum-soaked macaroon cookies. Chill at least 8 hours before serving. Garnish with whipped cream and pineapple spears.

Peach and Rum Shortcake Nests

Here is an attractive dessert for your Easter dinner. You'll find it easy to prepare with guests asking for your recipe.

I sometimes put a tablespoon of vanilla pudding or some sliced strawberries under the peach for a surprise. Mix your favorite rum drink for sipping.

2 tablespoons cornstarch
1 1/4 cups pineapple juice
1 tablespoon lemon juice
1 teaspoon grated lemon rind
1/4 cup light rum
yellow food coloring
8 individual sponge cake shells
8 peach halves
1/4 cup coconut

Mix cornstarch with pineapple juice in a saucepan until it dissolves. Add lemon juice, lemon rind, and rum and cook until it thickens. Sip and stir constantly as it cooks. Add a few drops of yellow food coloring for a brighter color. Cool. Place 1 tablespoon of pineapple glaze in each cake shell. These are the same cakes which are sold with strawberries when they are in season for shortcake. Top with a peach half with the cut side down. Have a sip of your drink and pour the pineapple glaze over the peach and the cake. Garnish the edge of the cake with coconut.

Rum Dums

It's cookie time again. Here is one Dad will want to share with his friends. If you can keep it stored for a few days, it improves with age. We like it for the holidays and gift giving, too. Let's sip on a Cuba Libre.

1 cup sugar
1 cup shortening
1 egg
3 tablespoons rum
2 1/4 cups sifted flour
1/2 cup chopped maraschino cherries
1 tablespoon juice from cherries
1/2 cup chopped nuts
1/2 cup white raisins
1/2 cup coconut

Blend sugar and shortening until smooth; add egg and stir in rum. Have a sip and mix in flour, cherries, juice, nuts, and raisins. Form dough into 2 rolls and roll in coconut. Chill for 3 hours and slice 1/4 inch thick. Place on ungreased cookie sheet. Bake at 375° for 12 minutes. Yield: 4 dozen.

Rum Snowballs

This cookie requires no baking so you retain the full value of the rum. It keeps well and should be stored at least five days before serving. (They improve with age.) If it's a cold day, make yourself a hot rum toddy to sip.

3 cups crushed vanilla wafers (8 ounces)
1 cup powdered sugar
3 tablespoons cocoa
1/4 teaspoon salt
1 cup nuts, chopped fine

1/4 cup light corn syrup
1/4 cup rum

Combine vanilla wafers, powdered sugar, cocoa, and salt in a large bowl. Stir in the rest of the ingredients and blend well. The mixture will be very stiff. Dust hands with powdered sugar and shape the dough into balls. Let stand uncovered for 1 hour. This will give you time to finish your hot rum toddy. One hour later roll the balls in powdered sugar and store for at least 5 days. No cooking required! Makes 5 dozen.

Second Piece

This is an old recipe that Aunt Violet called "Second Piece" because it was so good and tender that everyone asked for a second helping. The molasses and rum blend to produce a uniquely flavored cake.

1/2 cup butter
1 cup sugar
1 cup molasses
2 teaspoons baking soda
3/4 cup hot water
1/4 cup rum
2 1/2 cups flour
1 teaspoon cinnamon
1/2 teaspoon cloves
2 eggs, beaten

Mix butter and sugar until smooth, stir in molasses, baking soda, hot water, and rum. Add dry ingredients and mix well. Stir in the eggs. Spread batter into a greased 9 x 9 x 2" pan. Bake at 350° for 1 hour. Serve with whipped cream or lemon sauce.

Sour Cream Rum Cake

This is a rich, moist, delicately rum-flavored cake that makes any day a special occasion. I like sipping on a rum and Coke when I do the baking.

1/2 cup butter
1 cup sugar
3 eggs, separated
2 tablespoons grated lemon peel
2 cups sifted flour
1 teaspoon soda
1 teaspoon baking powder

1/4 teaspoon salt
1 cup sour cream
1 cup chopped nuts
1 cup chocolate chips

Topping:
1 cup powdered sugar
2 tablespoons orange juice
1 tablespoon lemon juice
2 tablespoons rum

After mixing your rum and Coke, check to be sure that you have all the ingredients and start by creaming the butter and sugar together. Beat in egg yolks and add the lemon peel. Have a sip and stir in the dry ingredients alternately with the sour cream. Beat egg whites until stiff and fold into the batter with the nuts and chocolate chips. Pour into a greased tube pan. Bake at 350° for 50 minutes. Combine topping ingredients. After removing cake from pan, punch full of holes and spread topping over cake while it is still warm.

Sugar Daddy Cake

Anybody's daddy will like this rum-spiced cake. It keeps well and is wonderful to have on hand to serve with coffee when someone drops by for a visit. Make it on a cold winter evening as you sip a hot rum toddy.

1/4 cup rum
1 cup raisins

2 tablespoons flour
2/3 cup candied fruit
1 cup butter
1 cup sugar
3 eggs, beaten
1/2 teaspoon salt
1 3/4 cups sifted cake flour
1 tablespoon baking powder
1 cup chopped nuts

Have a sip of your rum toddy and pour rum over the raisins. Let them soak as you mix the rest of the ingredients. Stir 2 tablespoons of flour into the candied fruits and set aside. While you have another sip, mix butter and sugar together in a large bowl. Stir in beaten eggs until batter is smooth. Add the raisins and rum mixture and the dry ingredients and mix well. Stir in nuts and fruits. Pour the batter into a greased loaf pan and bake at 325° for 1 hour.

Trinidad Nut Loaves

These rum flavored chocolate loaves are ideal to have at home. We use them for desserts, snacks, and gifts during the holidays. They are rich and cake-like in texture. If you are baking on a hot day, try sipping on a frozen daiquiri.

2 cups sugar
1 cup shortening
5 eggs
3 ounces unsweetened chocolate
1/4 cup rum

2 1/2 cups sifted cake flour
1 teaspoon baking soda
1 teaspoon salt
1 1/4 cups buttermilk
1 cup chopped almonds
1/2 cup raisins

Mix a frozen daiquiri and assemble the ingredients. Cream the sugar and shortening until smooth. Use an electric mixer if you have one. Add eggs one at a time, beating after each addition. Stir in chocolate and rum. Add the dry ingredients alternately with the buttermilk. Have a sip and stir in nuts and raisins. Pour into two greased loaf pans. Bake at 350° for 45 minutes. Cool before slicing. Serve with ice cream, whipped cream, or hard sauce.

7
Whiskey

CRAB COCKTAIL
JOHN BARLEY'S
SWISS STEAK
BLACK-EYED PEA
CASSEROLE
SOUTHERN BOURBON
PILAF RING
DOUBLE SCOTCH
MUFFINS
RYE DROP CAKES
TUTTI-FRUTTI
BOURBON DROPS
BOURBON-MOLASSES
DOUGHNUTS
BOURBON SNAPS
IRISH COFFEE
PUDDING
IRISH TRIFLE
GUMDROP-WHISKEY
CAKE
TIPSY CAKE
WHISKEY DROPS

Crab Cocktail

This is a first course appetizer for that special dinner you have been planning. The bourbon whiskey gives a unique flavor to the crab cocktail. Mix yourself a Whiskey Sour before you start dinner.

2 cups cooked crab
1 tablespoon lemon juice
2 cups chili sauce
1/2 teaspoon Tabasco sauce
1/2 teaspoon chili powder
2 tablespoons bourbon whiskey
1 cup chopped celery
2 hard-cooked eggs, sliced
1 lemon

Combine first 7 ingredients and chill well. Serve on lettuce or in cocktail dishes, garnishing with egg slices and a lemon wedge.

John Barley's Swiss Steak

The unique flavor of this dish comes from the bourbon and tomato combination. It is easy to prepare and makes a good oven meal with baked potatoes and stuffed zucchini. Sip on a bourbon highball as you work.

1/3 cup flour
2 teaspoons salt
1/4 teaspoon garlic salt
2 pounds round steak cut 1 1/2 inches thick
3 tablespoons shortening
1/4 cup bourbon

1 onion, sliced
1 can tomatoes, finely chopped (28 ounces)

Combine the flour and salts, rub into steak and cut into serving-size pieces. Have a sip and melt shortening in a heavy skillet; brown the steak slowly on both sides. Remove the steak and place in a baking dish. Add any remaining flour mixture to the meat drippings in the skillet. Have a sip and stir in bourbon, onion, and tomatoes with their juice. Simmer until thickened. Pour over the meat and cover with a lid or foil. Bake at 300° for 1 1/2 to 2 hours or until very tender. This gives you time for another drink as you prepare the rest of the dinner.

Black-Eyed Pea Casserole

This traditional Southern dish will soon become your favorite. It is always served on New Year's Day in the South to bring good luck throughout the coming year. This cooks for a long time so let's sip on a tall bourbon and 7-Up.

3 cups dried black-eyed peas
2 teaspoons salt
6 slices bacon, cut in pieces
1 quart water
1 cup barbecue sauce
1/4 cup bourbon
2 onions, chopped
1 tablespoon molasses
1/4 cup brown sugar

Wash peas; cover with water and soak overnight. Mix your highball and drain and rinse peas; combine with salt, bacon and water in a heavy saucepan. Cover and bring to a boil. Reduce heat and simmer 45 minutes or until peas are just tender. Sip and stir often. Add more water if necessary. Add barbecue sauce, bourbon, onions, molasses, and brown sugar. Cover and simmer 2 more hours. Mix another drink and stir occasionally. If peas become too dry, add more water. Serves 8. They taste even better the next day heated in a casserole and topped with cheese.

Southern Bourbon Pilaf Ring

Even your Northern friends will enjoy grits prepared in this manner. Use it as a potato or rice substitute for your next dinner. Let's sip on a Whiskey Sour as we plan our menu.

8 fresh mushrooms, medium size
2 tablespoons butter
1/2 cup onion, chopped
1 clove garlic, minced
1/4 cup parsley
2 3/4 cups chicken broth
1/4 cup bourbon
1/2 teaspoon salt
1/4 teaspoon thyme
1 1/2 cups grits

This takes quite a bit of chopping time; you may need another **Whiskey Sour** before you are finished. Grease the bottom of a ring mold, line with waxed paper, and grease the waxed paper. Slice mushrooms and sauté in the butter. Line the ring with the mushroom slices. Sauté onion and garlic with the rest of the mushrooms. Add parsley, broth, bourbon, salt, and thyme and bring to a boil. This gives you a chance for a sip before you slowly stir in the grits. Cook uncovered, stirring frequently, for 3 to 5 minutes. Spoon into the ring mold and let stand at room temperature for 15 minutes. Unmold and remove waxed paper. Serve immediately. This can be made ahead of time and stored in the refrigerator overnight. Place mold on a rack in a large pan and add water. Bring to a boil and steam 25 minutes, or use an electric steamer.

Double Scotch Muffins

This hot bread really does produce a double Scotch flavor. There is just enough Scotch whiskey in the recipe to complement the butterscotch flavor of the brown sugar. Try them for your next brunch or for a quiet supper that you are planning "just for him." Really be daring and sip a double Scotch as you cook!

2 cups packaged pancake mix
1/4 cup brown sugar
1/2 teaspoon salt
1 egg
1/2 cup milk
1/4 cup salad oil
1/4 cup Scotch
1/2 cup raisins
1/2 cup chopped nuts

Combine pancake mix, brown sugar, and salt in a large bowl. Beat egg, milk, and oil together and stir into the dry ingredients with a fork. Have a sip and stir in Scotch, raisins, and nuts. Fill greased muffin tins 2/3 full. Bake at 400° for 15 minutes or until done.

Rye Drop Cakes

This is an old recipe that my grandmother used for special occasions. We think you will find these rich little cakes a big hit at the breakfast table. Sip on your favorite drink as you prepare these old-fashioned breakfast cakes.

2/3 cup rye flour
2/3 cup sifted flour
1 tablespoon baking powder
1/2 teaspoon salt
1/4 cup milk
1/4 cup whiskey
2 tablespoons molasses
1 egg

Mix and sift dry ingredients together. Combine milk, whiskey, molasses, and beaten egg and add alternately to the dry ingredients. Drop by small spoonfuls into deep hot fat at 325°. Cook slowly until dark brown on all sides; turn as needed. Drain on a paper towel and serve warm with butter and maple syrup. Makes 18 cakes.

Bourbon Drops

Cookies are good any time. These bourbon flavored drop

cookies make a welcome gift during the holidays. Dad won't complain if you put them in his lunch box for a surprise. Let's sip on a bourbon highball as we cook.

1 cup sugar
1/2 cup shortening
1 egg, beaten
2 tablespoons milk
1/4 cup bourbon
1 1/2 cups sifted flour
1/2 teaspoon salt
1/2 teaspoon soda
1 teaspoon cinnamon
1/2 teaspoon cloves
1 1/2 cups rolled oats
1/2 cup nuts
1 cup raisins

Cream sugar and shortening until smooth. Stir in egg and have a sip of your drink. Combine milk and bourbon and stir into the mixture alternately with the dry ingredients. Mix in oats, nuts, and raisins until well blended. Drop by teaspoons onto a greased cookie sheet. Bake at 350° for 12 to 15 minutes as you finish your highball.

Bourbon-Molasses Doughnuts

If you have never made doughnuts, you will be surprised how easy they are to make. There is just enough bourbon in the batter to make the taster curious. Try freezing any leftovers. Mix a Manhattan and start sipping and stirring.

5 cups sifted flour
1 teaspoon salt
1 teaspoon baking soda
1/2 teaspoon cinnamon
1 teaspoon ginger
1 egg
3/4 cup molasses
1 cup buttermilk
1/4 cup bourbon
1 tablespoon salad oil
1/2 cup finely chopped nuts

Sift dry ingredients together in a large bowl. Have a sip of your Manhattan and beat the egg. Add the molasses, buttermilk, bourbon, and oil to the egg and mix well. Slowly stir into the dry ingredients. Stir in the nuts; you should have a soft dough. Have a sip and roll out on a well-floured board until 1/4 inch thick. Cut with a doughnut cutter. Fry in deep hot fat at 370° until brown; turn and cook until brown on both sides. Drain and dip in powdered sugar. Serve warm.

Bourbon Snaps

Watch Dad snap to attention when he bites into one of these crisp cookies. When he realizes the good flavor has a slight bourbon touch, he will probably check the bourbon bottle. If you do any extra sipping be sure to fill up his bottle.

3/4 cup sugar

140 / Sip and Stir

1 cup soft shortening
1 egg
1 cup walnuts, finely chopped
2 1/2 cups flour
1/4 teaspoon salt
1 teaspoon allspice
1 teaspoon ginger
2 teaspoons cinnamon
1/2 cup bourbon

Cream sugar and shortening together until smooth. Have a sip of your bourbon highball and stir in the egg. Combine nuts and 1 cup of flour and stir into the mixture. Add the rest of the dry ingredients alternately with the bourbon. Chill dough at least 1 hour. This is a good time to finish your drink. Roll dough about 1/4 inch thick and cut into circles or your favorite shape and sprinkle with sugar. Place on a greased cookie sheet and bake at 400° for 8 minutes. They should be slightly browned around the edges. Makes about 6 dozen cookies.

Irish Coffee Pudding

This is one of our fun desserts. We like to serve it on St. Patrick's Day but it is good anytime. Pick a cold day to cook so that you can really enjoy sipping on some Irish coffee. After mixing the pudding, I always spoon it into my Irish coffee glasses. If you don't have any, use **parfait** glasses or your favorite serving dish.

1 package chocolate whipped dessert mix

2 teaspoons instant coffee powder
1/2 cup cold milk
1/3 cup cold water
3 tablespoons Irish whiskey
1 cup whipping cream
1/2 cup chopped walnuts

Time to set down your Irish coffee and combine the dessert mix and coffee powder in a medium-sized bowl. Stir in the milk and beat with electric beater for 1 minute. Add water and whiskey and beat until fluffy. Have a sip of your Irish coffee and then whip cream until thick. Fold it into the dessert mixture and add nuts. Spoon into serving dishes and chill until set. Garnish with whipped cream, nuts, and shaved chocolate.

Irish Trifle

This is an excellent way to use up dry cake. Fix yourself

142 / Sip and Stir

a bourbon and water. Be sure to use bottled water if the water in your area has a bad mineral taste. Have a sip.

1 small sponge or pound cake
1 large can of fruit cocktail
1 package raspberry flavored gelatin (3 ounces)
1 1/3 cups water
1/3 cup juice
1/3 cup bourbon
1 package custard mix
1/2 cup whipping cream

Cut cake in 1/2 inch cubes and place one layer of cake on the bottom of a bowl. Drain fruit cocktail and reserve juice. Place half of fruit on cake, then another layer of cake and the remainder of the fruit. Set aside and have a sip of your drink. Dissolve gelatin in 1 cup boiling water. When dissolved, add 1/3 cup juice, 1/3 cup bourbon, and 1/3 cup cold water. Cool the mixture—this gives you time to finish your drink. When gelatin is cool, pour over cake and let set 30 minutes before refrigerating. This gives you time to fix another bourbon and water. When gelatin is set, add a layer of custard (make according to package directions) and finish with a layer of whipped cream.

Gumdrop-Whiskey Cake

Here is another recipe to add to your holiday collection. My family prefers it to the standard fruit cake. Make a double batch and give one to a friend. Try sipping on a Whiskey Sour as you bake this cake.

1 cup butter
2 cups sugar
2 eggs, beaten
1 cup applesauce
1/2 cup bourbon
4 cups sifted flour
1 teaspoon baking soda
1 teaspoon cinnamon
1/4 teaspoon nutmeg
1/2 teaspoon salt
1 1/2 pounds of small gumdrops
1 pound raisins
1 1/2 cups chopped walnuts

Blend butter and sugar together until smooth. Have a sip of your Whiskey Sour and stir in the eggs. Mix applesauce and bourbon together and add alternately with the dry ingredients. Have a sip and stir in gumdrops, raisins, and nuts. Grease two loaf pans and line the bottoms with waxed paper. Spoon the batter into the pan and bake at 325° for 1 hour while you mix another Whiskey Sour.

Tipsy Cake

This bourbon-laced holiday cake keeps well and is always a welcome gift. It is very rich and servings should be small. Sip on your favorite bourbon drink as you work in the kitchen.

1 cup butter
2 cups sugar

6 eggs
1/2 cup bourbon
4 cups sifted flour
1 teaspoon baking powder
3 teaspoons nutmeg
1 teaspoon cinnamon
3 cups chopped walnuts
1 pound raisins
1/2 pound sliced candied cherries
powdered sugar

    Blend sugar and butter until smooth. Add eggs one at a time and beat well after each addition. Have a sip of your drink. Add dry ingredients alternately with bourbon. Stir in nuts, raisins, and cherries. Pour batter into a greased 10-inch tube pan. Bake at 300° for 2 hours. This gives you time to mix another drink. Remove and let cool 15 minutes. Turn out on a rack and cool completely. Sprinkle with more bourbon and wrap in foil. Let cake age at least a week. Moisten with bourbon 2 or 3 more times. Sprinkle with powdered sugar before slicing and serving.

Tutti-Frutti Whiskey Drops

    Here is another cookie recipe to add to your Christmas collection. It stores well and the flavor improves with age. These tasty cookie drops are a welcome gift anytime. Mix a bourbon highball and start sipping.

1 cup brown sugar
1/4 cup butter

2 eggs
1 1/2 teaspoons soda dissolved in 2 teaspoons milk
1 1/2 cups sifted flour
1/4 teaspoon cloves
1/2 teaspoon nutmeg
1/2 teaspoon cinnamon
1/4 cup each, candied cherries, orange peel, and lemon peel
1/4 cup chopped candied pineapple
1 cup raisins
1/4 cup bourbon
1 cup chopped pecans

Cream the sugar and butter until smooth; add eggs one at a time and beat well. Add the dissolved soda and have a sip. Sift the flour and spices together and add to the candied fruits and raisins. Mix well and stir into the sugar mixture. Mix bourbon in slowly and fold in the nuts. Drop from a teaspoon onto a greased cookie sheet. You have time for a refill now if you're ready. Bake at 300° for 20 minutes.

# 8
Vodka and Gin

CHEESE LOG
SALMON ON THE ROCKS
SPEAKEASY
  CHEESE BALL
TOMATO ROCKER
SHRIMP COCKTAIL
BOOTLEGGER CHICKEN
CRAB PILAF
SPIKED PEACH

FIREWATER SWORDFISH
FLAMING GAME HENS
SPIKED HAM AND
  CHEESE SANDWICHES
ZINGY CHICKEN WITH
  DUMPLINGS
MARGARITA PIE
SCREWDRIVER TARTS
COFFEE CAKE

Cheese Log

Make a Vodka Gibson to sip on while you make this cheese log for tomorrow night's party.

1 package cream cheese (8 ounces)
1/4 cup soy sauce
2 tablespoons vodka
1/4 cup toasted sesame seeds

Punch cream cheese full of holes. Have a sip and pour the soy sauce and vodka over the cheese and marinate overnight. Roll the cheese in the toasted sesame seeds. Garnish with parsley. This is very easy and is delicious served with an assortment of crackers.

Salmon on the Rocks

This is a vodka-inspired spread for party snacks. It is mixed in a blender and is better if refrigerated for several hours before serving. We sip vodka martinis while we are mixing and later when we are sampling the hors d'oeuvres.

1 cup cottage cheese
1 can salmon, drained
1/4 cup vodka
2 tablespoons chili sauce
1/2 onion, chopped
1 tablespoon chives
1/4 teaspoon salt
1/4 teaspoon Tabasco sauce

We could call this a "3 sip recipe" because it is made so quickly. First sip you assemble the ingredients; second sip is putting ingredients in the blender and you take the third sip as you blend them for 30 seconds or until smooth. Spoon into a serving dish and garnish with parsley and you're ready to mix another martini!

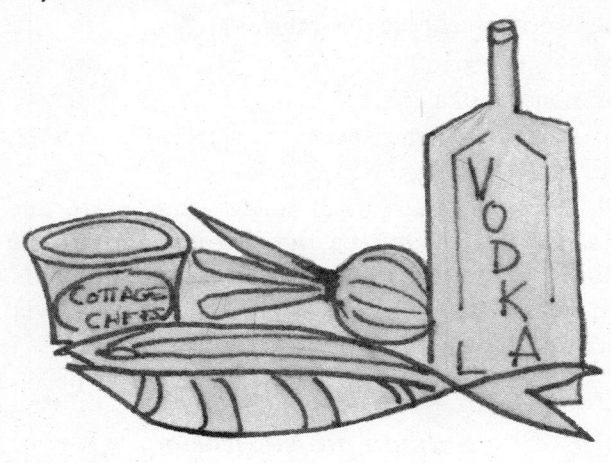

Speakeasy Cheese Ball

When it's time for that next "TGIF" party, speak up and volunteer to bring this cheese ball. You can sip on gin and tonic as you prepare it the night before the party. The three cheeses combine to produce a tasty ball.

1 package cream cheese (8 ounces)
5 ounces processed sharp cheddar cheese spread
5 ounces processed blue cheese spread
1 tablespoon gin
1 teaspoon wine vinegar
1/8 teaspoon garlic salt
1 cup chopped pecans

Allow cheeses to soften to room temperature. Combine cheeses, gin, wine vinegar, and garlic salt. Beat until smooth, then refrigerate at least 30 minutes to make cheese easier to handle. Shape cheese into a ball and roll in chopped nuts. (This is really better if made at least one day in advance.)

Tomato Rocker Shrimp Cocktail

On a hot summer day surprise your guests with this frozen shrimp cocktail. Sip on a Bloody Mary in the morning as you prepare the tomato juice mixture for the freezer. This attractive meal starter should be prepared hours before serving, be well chilled, and garnished attractively.

1 quart tomato juice
2 teaspoons lemon juice
1/2 cup vodka
1/2 teaspoon Tabasco sauce
1/2 cup dairy sour cream
1/2 teaspoon onion salt
24 shelled cooked medium shrimps
1 tablespoon chopped parsley
crisp greens

Have a sip of your Bloody Mary and combine tomato juice, lemon juice, vodka, and Tabasco sauce. Pour mixture into an ice tray and freeze until mushy, stirring now and then. Freeze until firm. Combine sour cream and onion salt. Cover and refrigerate until ready to assemble cocktails. Line icers or cocktail glasses with greens. Fill each with about

1/2 cup of the frozen tomato ice. Top with 1 tablespoon of the sour cream dressing and garnish with 3 shrimps and parsley. Makes 8 servings.

Bootlegger Chicken

This oven-baked chicken dish will become a family and company favorite. Children will like the peaches and Mom will like the easy way it goes together. Sip on a Vodka Collins as you prepare this attractive dish.

6 tablespoons flour
1 teaspoon salt
1/4 teaspoon pepper
1 teaspoon paprika
1 large fryer, cut in serving pieces
1/4 cup butter
1/2 cup slivered almonds
1 cup beef broth
2 tablespoons vodka
2 tablespoons ketchup
1/2 cup dairy sour cream
1 can peach halves, drained (16 ounces)
1/2 cup Parmesan cheese

Mix flour, salt, pepper, and paprika; dredge chicken in mixture and reserve any remaining flour. Have a sip as you brown chicken in butter. Remove chicken to a 2-quart casserole dish and lightly brown almonds in the drippings. Stir in remaining flour mixture. Stir in broth and vodka gradually. Add ketchup and cook, stirring until thick. Remove from heat and stir in sour cream. Pour over chicken, cover and bake in oven at 375° for 40 minutes. Arrange peaches, cut side up, on and around chicken and sprinkle with cheese. Return to oven uncovered for 10 minutes.

Crab Pilaf

Here is a vitamin-packed casserole that provides fish, cheese, and rice in one dish. All are important nutrients to us during our busy days of work and play. Try sipping on a gin and tonic as you work in the kitchen.

1 cup rice, uncooked
1 tablespoon instant onions
1 envelope dry chicken noodle soup
1/2 cup butter or margarine
2 1/4 cups water
1/4 cup gin
1/4 cup cheddar cheese, grated
1 can crabmeat (6 1/2 ounces)

Brown rice, onions, and noodles (from the soup envelope) in the butter as you sip on your gin and tonic. Boil 2 1/4 cups of water; add broth cube from the soup envelope and the gin. Add boiling water mixture to rice. Add cheese and crab and stir until cheese melts. Simmer for 30 minutes. If you prefer, put in a shallow casserole, cover, and bake at 325° for 30 minutes as you finish your drink.

152 / Sip and Stir

Firewater Swordfish

4 swordfish steaks
2 tablespoons lemon juice
1/4 teaspoon garlic powder
2 tablespoons soy sauce
1 tablespoon sugar
1/2 cup vodka
2 tablespoons diced onions

Pour a small glass of vodka with orange juice. This recipe is so easy you'll only have time for a few sips. Combine all the ingredients in a bowl and stir until sugar dissolves. Brush the marinade on the fish steaks and refrigerate for at least 4 hours. Broil 4 inches from the heat for about 10 minutes. Baste with the marinade. It should be lightly browned on both sides. Before starting to broil have another Screwdriver. If the mercury content is too high in the swordfish in your area, substitute any solid-type fish such as halibut or flounder.

Flaming Game Hens

This is an easy and elegant company dish. It can be prepared ahead of time and cooked while you are getting ready for the party. The flaming fruits produce a dramatic garnish to a meal that will be long remembered.

4 cornish game hens
3 cups cooked rice
1 teaspoon salt
1 egg
1/4 cup grated celery
1/4 cup grated onion
1/4 cup vodka
2 tablespoons chopped parsley
1/2 cup slivered almonds
1/2 cup wine jelly or apricot jelly
1 banana
1 cup pineapple chunks (fresh or canned)
4 maraschino cherries

Let's sip on a Vodka Collins as we prepare the stuffing for the birds. Combine rice, salt, egg, celery, onion, vodka, parsley, and almonds in a bowl and mix well. Wash birds and clean out cavity. Rub with butter and fill with the rice stuffing; fasten with a toothpick. Bake at 350° for 1 hour. Baste during the last 30 minutes of the baking time with the jelly. On a toothpick alternate layers of banana and pineapple topping them with a cherry. Marinate in 100 proof vodka for at least 30 minutes. When ready to serve, stick toothpick into the breast of the cooked game hen and ignite.

Spiked Ham and Cheese Sandwiches

Sandwiches are good anytime; surprise guests and serve this grilled sandwich some morning for breakfast. Don't be surprised if Dad asks you to make it again soon. Try sipping on tomato juice with just a little bit of gin.

8 slices bread
butter
prepared mustard
4 slices boiled ham
4 slices cheddar cheese
1 tomato, sliced
2 slightly beaten eggs
2 tablespoons gin
1 cup crushed potato chips

Spread each slice of bread on one side with butter and then with mustard. Top with ham, cheese, tomato slices and the rest of the bread. Have a sip, combine eggs and gin, and beat together. Crush potato chips with a rolling pin. Dip sandwiches in egg mixture, then in crushed potato chips. Coat sandwich with chips on both sides. Melt butter in a skillet and brown the sandwiches on both sides until crisp. It will take about 10 minutes. Serve hot.

Zingy Chicken with Dumplings

Chicken casserole is good any time, but is ideal for Sunday afternoon supper. A fruit gelatin salad and fresh green vegetable with Dad's favorite dessert will please the whole family. Mix a gin and tonic and get busy!

1 fryer cut in serving pieces or 6 breasts
1/4 cup butter
12 boiling onions
1/2 cup fresh mushrooms
1/2 teaspoon thyme
1 teaspoon salt
1 can cream of chicken soup
1 1/2 cups chicken broth
1/2 cup gin

Dumplings:
1 egg
1/2 cup milk
1 1/2 cups sifted flour
2 1/2 teaspoons baking powder
1/2 teaspoon salt
1 teaspoon poppy seeds

Brown chicken in butter in a frying pan. Remove the

chicken and place it in a Dutch oven. Add onions, mushrooms, seasonings, soup, chicken broth, and gin to the frying pan in which the chicken was browned. Simmer for 10 minutes as you sip your drink; pour sauce over the chicken. Bake at 375° for 1 hour. Combine egg and milk and stir in dry ingredients; mix well. Drop by teaspoons around the edge of chicken. Sprinkle with seeds, cover and simmer for 15 minutes.

Margarita Pie

Here is a new and different pie that was developed by the Sunkist Growers test kitchens. They were happy to have us include it in our book. We know you will be happy, too, as you sip on a Margarita. It's great with any meal, but really super as a climax to a Mexican dinner.

Pretzel Crumb Crust:
3/4 cup finely crushed pretzel crumbs (or 6 tablespoons each pretzel crumbs and crushed vanilla wafers)
3 tablespoons sugar
5 tablespoons melted butter or margarine

Use a rolling pin to crush pretzels. Have a sip of your Margarita. Combine crumbs and sugar; add butter gradually, stirring to mix well. Reserve 2 tablespoons for garnish. Press remaining mixture onto bottom and sides of well-buttered 9-inch pie plate; chill.

Margarita Cocktail Filling:
1 envelope unflavored gelatin
1 teaspoon grated lemon peel
7 tablespoons freshly squeezed lemon juice

4 egg yolks
1/2 cup sugar
1/4 teaspoon salt
5 tablespoons tequila
2 tablespoons plus 2 teaspoons Triple Sec
5 egg whites
7 tablespoons sugar
1 Sunkist lemon, unpeeled, thinly sliced into cartwheels

Soften gelatin in mixture of lemon peel and juice for 5 minutes. Beat egg yolks in top of double boiler until very thick; beat in 1/2 cup sugar and salt. Add gelatin mixture and cook over boiling water, stirring constantly, until slightly thickened and gelatin is dissolved, about 7 minutes. This is a good time to sip. Immediately transfer to bowl; thoroughly blend in liquors. Chill over ice water or in refrigerator, stirring frequently until just cold to the touch. (Mixture should not be too thick.) Meanwhile, beat egg whites just to *soft* peak stage; gradually beat in 7 tablespoons of sugar at high speed until all sugar is used. Whites should be glossy and moist and tips of peaks should fall over slightly when beater is withdrawn. Carefully fold yolk mixture, about 1/3 at a time, into whites. Spoon into chilled Pretzel Crumb Crust; sprinkle with reserved crumbs. Prepare lemon slices for "twists;" arrange around edge of pie. Chill until firm. Best when served the same day it is made. Isn't it pretty? We think you've earned another Margarita.

Screwdriver Tarts

Here is a dessert that you can't help but enjoy making. We have used some convenience foods to cut preparation time down to a minimum, but the results are still outstanding. Start by sectioning 9 oranges. If you haven't sectioned an orange before be sure you have a sharp knife and the job is half done. Place oranges in a bowl and pour 1/4 cup of vodka over the oranges; let marinate about 1 hour. Now that you have the vodka out make yourself a Screwdriver for sipping.

9 oranges, sectioned
1/4 cup vodka
1 package vanilla pudding and pie filling mix
8 baked tart shells
1/2 cup sugar
1 1/2 tablespoons cornstarch
1 cup water
2 teaspoons grated orange peel
1 tablespoon lemon juice
few drops of orange food coloring

Prepare pudding mix according to package directions; chill until cool but not set. Spoon about 1/4 cup filling into each tart shell; chill. In a saucepan combine sugar and cornstarch; blend in water until smooth. Bring to a boil and boil for 3 minutes. Stir in grated orange peel, lemon juice, and food coloring; cool slightly. Put orange sections and vodka into a large sieve over a bowl. Make another Screwdriver out of any juice that drains from the marinated sections. Pour warm glaze over the orange sections several times, allowing glaze to drain through the sieve until all sections are coated. Arrange glazed sections on chilled tarts; spoon 1 tablespoon of glaze on each; chill.

Spiked Peach Coffee Cake

This coffee cake is for special occasions only. I use it for Easter and anniversary breakfasts. The apricot jam and brandy topping creates a glistening glaze. Gin and tonic is a good drink to sip as you make this.

1 cup sifted flour
1 1/2 teaspoons baking powder
1/2 teaspoon salt
1 tablespoon sugar
1/4 cup shortening
1 egg
1/4 cup milk
1/4 cup gin
3 peaches, thinly sliced
1/2 teaspoon cinnamon
1/4 teaspoon nutmeg
2 tablespoons sugar
2 tablespoons butter, melted
1/2 cup apricot jam
1 teaspoon apricot brandy

Combine the first 4 ingredients. Cut in shortening with a pastry blender. Stir in egg, milk, and gin with a fork—batter will be lumpy. Spread into a greased baking dish. Arrange peaches in parallel rows on top. Sprinkle with cinnamon, nutmeg, and sugar. Top with butter. Bake at 400° for 30 to 40 minutes. Beat jam and brandy together and spread on top.

9
Brandies and Liqueurs

ONION-CHEESE SOUP
MANDARIN CRAB SALAD
MINT MIST
HAM À GLO
ITALIAN BAKED FISH
  AND CARROTS
MINT-GLAZED PEAS
PINEAPPLE BEETS
SWEET POTATOES À LA
  ORANGE
APPLE BRANDY
  WAFFLES WITH
  HARD CIDER SAUCE
APRICOT-WALNUT
  BREAD
ISLAND TOAST WITH
  ORANGE CURACAO
  SYRUP
MINCEMEAT MUFFINS

APRICOT BRANDY CAKE
CHERRY BOMBS
CITRUS CUPCAKES
CRÈME DE CACAO BALLS
CRÈME DE MENTHE
  BROWNIES
CURACAO CO-CO PIE
FLAMING BANANAS
FROZEN MOCHA PIE
GRASSHOPPER PIE
INDIVIDUAL
  CHEESECAKES
KAHLUA CREAM PUFFS
MICKEY FINN
  PINEAPPLE
ORANGE GEMS
PEACHES AND
  CREAM MOLD
ROCKY ROAD COOKIES

Onion-Cheese Soup

If it's cold outside, this soup will really hit the spot. The smell of it cooking should bring a crowd to your kitchen. We like it for lunch with a sandwich or as a special first course for company dinner.

2 large onions, sliced
3 tablespoons butter
5 cups beef bouillon
1/4 teaspoon ginger
1/2 teaspoon salt
4 ounces cheddar cheese, grated
1/4 cup brandy
4 slices French bread, cut in cubes
2 tablespoons chopped parsley

Maybe just a sniff of brandy to get started? The onions will probably make you cry so you will need a sip or two when you finish that job! Sauté the onions in a large frying pan in the melted butter until brown. Add the bouillon, ginger, and salt; simmer for 45 minutes. Use 1 bouillon cube to 1 cup water. Stir the grated cheese into the soup until it melts and add the brandy. Serve the soup topped with bread cubes and garnished with parsley and finish your brandy.

Mandarin Crab Salad

This is an elegant and different salad to serve to the girls at lunch. It is really a ladies dish; the men will eat

162 / Sip and Stir

it, but usually want something more substantial. The Grand Marnier's subtle flavor accents the mandarin oranges. When they are in season, I use fresh tangeloes instead. They are from the tangerine family also.

1/2 pound fresh crabmeat
1 can mandarin oranges
2 teaspoons Grand Marnier
1/2 cup celery, diced
2 tablespoons onion, chopped
1/4 cup Thousand Island dressing
salt to taste
lettuce

Pour a pony of Grand Marnier and let's get the salad made! It is strong, so make your sips small. Combine all the ingredients and mix with the Thousand Island dressing. Serve cold on lettuce leaves. Garnish with parsley and a twist of lemon. For a luncheon serve it with hot rolls, iced tea, and your favorite cake. If you don't have one, try the apple wine cake in this book.

Mint Mist

Cooking pork roast or pork chops tonight? Try this mint-accented gelatin salad as an accompaniment. This salad complements almost any meat, especially pork. I like to add a few drops of green food coloring to make it a pale green color. Let's start sipping some crème de menthe on the rocks.

1 can crushed pineapple (20 ounces)
1 cup pineapple juice
1 envelope unflavored gelatin
1/3 cup apple jelly
2 tablespoons crème de menthe
1 cup heavy cream, whipped

Drain the pineapple and reserve the juice. Soften gelatin in 1/2 cup of pineapple juice. Place over low heat, stirring constantly until gelatin dissolves. You can sip on your drink as you do this. Remove from the heat and add jelly and crème de menthe; stir until smooth. Add pineapple and the remainder of juice. Have a sip and chill until slightly thickened. Fold in cream and pour into a lightly oiled 1-quart mold. Chill until set.

Ham À Glo

If you are in the mood for something that looks and tastes elegant, try this ham dish. Start sipping on a small glass of port wine.

3 center slices of smoked ham
1/4 cup melted margarine
1/4 teaspoon dry mustard
1/8 teaspoon ground cloves
1/4 cup margarine
1 can pitted dark sweet cherries
3/4 cup port wine
1/4 teaspoon powdered ginger

2 tablespoons grated orange rind
1/4 cup slivered almonds
2 tablespoons cornstarch mixed with 1/4 cup water to make a paste
1/4 cup cherry brandy, warmed

Brush the ham on both sides with a mixture of the melted margarine, mustard, and cloves. Place the ham in a shallow baking dish. Bake at 350° for 35 minutes or until the ham slices are lighty browned. Have another sip of wine before we begin the sauce. Drain the cherries and add the juice to the margarine in a saucepan. Add port, ginger, orange rind, and almonds. Stir in cornstarch mixture and cook until thickened. Fold in the cherries and sip on your port as you stir this for about 5 minutes. Remove ham from the oven and place on a serving platter. Pour brandy over sauce and set aflame. Spoon flaming sauce over the ham slices. Serves 4 to 6.

Italian Baked Fish

Save this recipe until your husband catches that big one. It can be used with almost any fish. We have tried it with mountain trout and barracuda from the ocean.

2 pounds fish fillets
1 teaspoon grated lemon peel
2 tablespoons lemon juice
1 tablespoon Grand Marnier
2 cups chopped tomatoes
1/2 teaspoon oregano
1/2 cup green pepper, diced

1/4 cup grated Parmesan cheese

Mix a tall, cool Red Lion especially if you have been out in the sun fishing all day. Clean the fish—don't wait for your husband to do it—and arrange the fish in a baking dish. Sprinkle grated lemon peel over the fish. Mix lemon juice and Grand Marnier together and pour over the fish. Let it stand while you prepare the rest of the ingredients. First have a sip and then finely chop the tomatoes and combine with oregano and green pepper. Spread over the fish and sprinkle the cheese on top. Bake at 375° for 30 minutes. If you were lucky enough to catch one larger than 2 pounds, have another drink and bake it 20 minutes more or until fish is firm and flaky. Garnish with parsley and lemon twists.

Mint-Glazed Peas and Carrots

Tired of fixing the same old vegetables. Try this recipe with your family some night and we are sure you will put it on your company list. The subtle mint flavor enhances both the peas and the carrots. I like to sip my crème de menthe on the rocks.

4 carrots, cut in strips
2 cups fresh peas
1/4 cup butter
1/4 teaspoon salt
1/4 cup sugar
1 tablespoon crème de menthe
2 tablespoons chopped parsley

Cook carrots in boiling water until tender, about 20 minutes. Take a sip of crème de menthe. Cook the peas in boiling water for 10 minutes. Add the peas to the cooked carrots. Combine the butter, salt, sugar, and crème de menthe in a saucepan and cook and stir until the butter melts and the sugar dissolves. Pour over the cooked vegetables and toss lightly. Sprinkle with chopped parsley as you finish your drink.

Pineapple Beets

This is a good vegetable to serve with pork chops or pork roast. It is colorful and the fruit complements the pork. It can be prepared ahead of time and reheated if you're planning a guest meal. Let's sip on a Red Lion. All you need is 3/4 ounce Grand Marnier, 3/4 ounce gin, 1 tablespoon lemon juice, and 2 tablespoons orange juice. Mix in a shaker and pour over ice.

1 tablespoon cornstarch
2 tablespoons brown sugar
2 tablespoons Grand Marnier
1 cup pineapple tidbits with syrup
1/4 teaspoon salt
1 tablespoon butter
1 tablespoon lemon juice
1 can sliced beets, drained (1 pound)

Are you enjoying your Red Lion? Combine cornstarch, sugar, Grand Marnier, and pineapple in a saucepan. Cook and stir until it thickens and boils. Add salt, butter, lemon juice, and beets; cook and sip until well heated.

Sweet Potatoes À La Orange

Make yourself a Gloom Chaser by stirring with ice 1/4 each of Grand Marnier, curacao, lemon juice, and grenadine. Strain and start sipping.

2 tablespoons butter
1/4 cup Grand Marnier
1/2 cup brown sugar
dash of salt
1 can vacuum-packed sweet potatoes (17 ounces)

Heat butter, Grand Marnier, brown sugar, and salt in a skillet. Simmer for 5 minutes. Carefully remove potatoes from can and place in skillet with sauce; turn to coat potatoes with the sauce and heat for 10 minutes, basting frequently. Serves 4.

Apple Brandy Waffles with Hard Cider Sauce

Here is a Sunday brunch dish which is good all year, especially in the fall when apples are in season and the mornings are crisp. Be sure your waffle iron is hot before pouring in the batter so that they will not stick. Fall is also a good time for apple brandy or hard cider sipping.

1 3/4 cups sifted flour
2 1/2 teaspoons baking powder
1/2 teaspoon salt
1 tablespoon sugar
2 eggs separated

5 tablespoons salad oil
3/4 cup milk
1/4 cup apple brandy
2 apples, peeled and sliced
1/4 cup chopped walnuts

This apple brandy really tastes good. Mix all the dry ingredients in a large bowl. Combine egg yolks, milk, oil, and brandy and beat together. Have a sip and stir the liquid mixture into the dry ingredients. Add the apple and nuts and mix well. Beat egg whites until stiff and fold into the batter. Bake in a hot waffle iron.

Hard Cider Sauce:
1 cup hard cider
1 cup brown sugar
1/4 teaspoon cinnamon
1/8 teaspoon nutmeg
1 teaspoon lemon juice
1/4 cup butter

Combine all ingredients in a saucepan and bring to a boil. Simmer for 15 minutes and serve hot.

Apricot-Walnut Bread

We have always had an apricot tree at home and an abundance of fresh apricots during July. My mother is busy making jams, jellies, cobblers, pies, and my favorite nut bread. We tried it this year with apricot brandy and like it better. Fill your cordial glass with brandy and sip slowly as you prepare this quick bread.

3/4 cup sugar
1 egg
3/4 cup milk
3 1/3 cups prepared biscuit mix
3/4 cup chopped walnuts
1 cup finely chopped fresh apricots
1/4 cup apricot brandy

After a sip or two get out a large bowl and mix sugar and egg together. Add milk and biscuit mix and beat until well blended. Have a sip and stir in nuts, apricots, and apricot brandy until thoroughly mixed. Spread batter into two small greased loaf pans. Bake at 350° for 50 minutes or until done. Let cool in pans 10 minutes while you finish your brandy, then turn out on cooling rack and let them cool completely.

Island Toast with Orange Curacao Syrup

This is a breakfast or brunch dish made for company. We like it served with fresh pineapple, ham slices, and hot coffee. Try it on New Year's day before the football marathon begins.

3 eggs, beaten
1/2 cup pineapple juice
2 tablespoons apricot brandy

1/2 cup dry bread crumbs
1/4 cup coconut
3 tablespoons butter
8 slices bread

For before-breakfast sipping try 1 cup of apricot nectar mixed with 1 tablespoon of apricot brandy. This is also a good juice to serve at brunch. Combine eggs, pineapple juice, and apricot brandy and mix well. Mix the bread crumbs and coconut together. Melt the butter in a large skillet. Have a sip of your apricot brandy drink and dip the bread in the pineapple-egg mixture and then in the bread crumb mixture. Brown on both sides.

Orange Curacao Syrup:
1 cup brown sugar
1/2 cup orange juice
1/4 cup curacao
2 teaspoons grated orange rind

Combine all the ingredients and simmer for 10 minutes. Serve hot on the Island Toast.

Mincemeat Muffins

This is a hearty quick bread that will be a welcome addition to any meal from breakfast to dinner. Try it with a big salad for lunch. The curacao creates a unique flavor. Pour a small glass and plan your menu.

1 1/2 cups corn meal

1/2 cup sifted flour
1 tablespoon baking powder
1/2 teaspoon salt
1/4 cup sugar
1/2 cup prepared mincemeat
3/4 cup milk
1/4 cup vegetable oil
1 egg, beaten
1/4 cup curacao

It's time to stop sipping and start working. Sift together the corn meal, flour, baking powder, salt, and sugar into a large bowl. Stir in the mincemeat; combine milk, oil, egg, and curacao. Have a sip and stir until dry ingredients are moistened; do not overbeat. Grease and fill muffin tins 3/4 full. Bake at 425° for 15 to 20 minutes or until brown. Serve hot.

Apricot Brandy Cake

This is an old-time "one-two-three-four cake." Just follow the numbers . . .

2 2/3 cups sifted cake flour
2 1/4 teaspoons baking powder
1/2 teaspoon salt
2 cups sugar
1 cup shortening
4 eggs, separated
2 tablespoons lemon extract

172 / Sip and Stir

3/4 cup apricot nectar
1/4 cup apricot brandy
2 cups powdered sugar
juice of 2 lemons

1. *Sift* flour with baking powder and salt and set aside.
2. *Cream* sugar and shortening together until very light. Add egg yolks one at a time, beating after each addition. Add lemon extract, apricot nectar, and brandy alternately with the dry ingredients.
3. *Stir* until smooth after each addition. Whip egg whites until stiff but not dry.
4. *Fold* egg whites lightly into the batter. Bake in a greased, floured tube pan for 1 hour at 350°.

While the cake is baking, sip on your brandy and sometime during the hour mix powdered sugar with the lemon juice. Set aside and when the cake is done, remove from the oven and pour the lemon-sugar mixture over the top of the cake at once. Let it cool in the pan thoroughly before removing.

Cherry Bombs

This is a Fourth of July spectacular. We like to make it after dinner and sip the Cherry Heering used to marinate the cherries. Then they will be ready for a picnic the next day and you will be too! You should have drained the cherries and filled the bottle with cherry liqueur yesterday. They are best if marinated for about 24 hours.

1 cup butter

1/2 cup powdered sugar
2 tablespoons honey
2 1/4 cups sifted flour
1/4 teaspoon salt
2 teaspoons cherry liqueur
3/4 cup finely chopped walnuts
40 maraschino cherries with stems

Put your Cherry Heering down and cream the butter and powdered sugar together until smooth. Stir in the honey and add the flour, salt, cherry liqueur, and nuts. This is a very stiff dough and you may want to put your glass down and mix the dough with your hands to blend it well. Drain the cherries and be sure to save the marinade for future use. Form the dough into balls around each cherry with the stem sticking out for the fuse to the bomb. Refrigerate for 1 hour. Place on a greased cookie sheet and bake at 375° for 15 minutes. While still warm roll in powdered sugar. Cool and roll in powdered sugar again. The result is 40 safe cherry bombs to take to a Fourth of July Picnic!

Citrus Cupcakes

This delightful cupcake originated in California where oranges are plentiful. We top ours with a plain white butter frosting and orange sections. It tastes equally good with a rich fudge frosting. Try sipping on a glass of orange juice mixed with a jigger of orange curacao.

1/2 cup shortening
1 cup sugar
2 eggs, beaten

1/4 cup orange juice
1 tablespoon orange curacao
2 cups sifted flour
1 1/2 teaspoons baking powder
1/2 teaspoon salt
3/4 cup milk
2 tablespoons grated orange rind
1/2 cup chopped pecans

Put down your orange drink and cream together shortening and sugar. Add eggs. Mix orange juice and liqueur together and add with half the dry ingredients and mix well. Stir in milk and the rest of the dry ingredients and beat until smooth. Stir in orange rind and nuts. Have a sip of your drink and spoon batter into greased muffin tins and bake at 350° for 25 minutes.

Crème De Cacao Balls

This is a baked version of the ball cookies. You can use crème de menthe or a cherry liqueur for variety if you make them for gift giving during the holidays. Sip on your favorite liqueur as you cook.

1 cup semi-sweet chocolate chips
1/2 cup shortening
1/2 cup brown sugar
1 egg
1 tablespoon crème de cacao
1 1/4 cups sifted flour
1/2 teaspoon baking soda

1/2 teaspoon salt
1 cup rolled oats

Melt chocolate chips and shortening together. Remove from heat and stir in brown sugar, egg, and crème de cacao. Have a sip and add the dry ingredients. Add oats and mix well. Have a sip before shaping the dough into walnut-sized balls. Place on ungreased cookie sheet and bake at 350° for 8 minutes. Roll in powdered sugar while warm. Yield: 4 dozen.

Crème De Menthe Brownies

This is a rich, moist chocolate bar cookie with a fresh mint flavor. We like it after dinner for those with a "sweet tooth." For after dinner sipping, it's hard to beat crème de menthe on the rocks.

4 ounces unsweetened chocolate
1 cup butter
2 cups sugar
2 eggs
2 teaspoons crème de menthe
1 cup sifted flour
1/4 teaspoon salt
1 cup chopped walnuts

Melt chocolate and butter together and remove from heat. Have a sip of your crème de menthe and add sugar, eggs, and crème de menthe. Add dry ingredients and mix well. Stir in nuts. Pour into a greased 9-inch square pan. Bake at 350° for 45 minutes. Cool and cut into squares.

Curacao Co-Co Pie

Make yourself a Biarritz Cocktail with 1/2 ounce of orange curacao, 2 ounces of brandy, and the juice of 1/2 lime. Mix and pour over ice. While you have the orange curacao out, let's make a pie:

1 9-inch pie shell, baked
1 2/3 cups orange juice
2 small packages of orange flavored gelatin
1/3 cup orange curacao
1 pint of vanilla ice cream, softened
1 can mandarin oranges, drained
1 package chocolate flavored whipped dessert mix
1/2 cup cream, whipped for a garnish

Heat the orange juice to boiling in a saucepan; remove from the heat and dissolve the gelatin in the juice. Now add the orange curacao and slowly add the ice cream. When the mixture is smooth, chill until the consistency of a milk shake (about 25 minutes). When chilled, add the mandarin orange slices, saving 6 for garnish and pour into a pastry shell. This will take some time so sit down and finish your drink.

You are now ready to make the chocolate dessert mix. Follow the directions on the back of the package. It will call for milk and/or water, depending on the brand that you select. Chill until the consistency of a milk shake. Spoon over the orange layer and chill several hours. Just before serving garnish with whipped cream and orange slices.

Flaming Bananas

This dish is prepared in a chafing dish and is taken to the table flaming. If you do not have a chafing dish, you will get the same results in an electric skillet. We will be sipping on a Brandy Alexander as we work.

4 firm ripe bananas
1/2 cup flour
1/4 cup butter
1/4 cup brown sugar
1/2 teaspoon cinnamon
1/4 teaspoon nutmeg
1/4 cup crème de cacao
2 tablespoons brandy, warmed
vanilla ice cream
1/4 cup finely chopped pecans

Peel bananas and slice lengthwise. Dust lightly with flour. Melt butter in chafing dish and add the brown sugar and spices. Sip and stir until the sugar is dissolved. Place bananas in the hot bubbling mixture. Spoon sauce over the bananas until they are well coated. Add the crème de cacao and cook for 1 minute. Add the brandy and ignite. When the flame dies, serve the bananas with the sauce, topped with a scoop of vanilla ice cream and chopped nuts.

Frozen Mocha Pie

The flavors of coffee and chocolate blend together in this frozen dessert and are spiced with a coffee liqueur.

Sip and Stir

You will find that it goes together very easily as you sip Kahlua.

24 chocolate wafers, finely crushed
1/4 cup butter, melted
1/4 cup Kahlua
1 jar marshmallow creme (7 ounces)
2 cups heavy cream, whipped

Toss the cookie crumbs with the melted butter, mixing well. Save 1/2 cup of the cookie crumbs for the top of your pie; press the rest into the bottom of a 9-inch pie pan or a spring-form pan. Have a sip and gradually add the Kahlua to the marshmallow creme and mix well. Fold the whipped cream into the marshmallow mixture and pour into the crumb-lined pan. Sprinkle the reserved crumbs around the edge and in the center of the pie. Freeze until firm—several hours.

Grasshopper Pie

Grasshopper Pie is a good dessert to make for a heavy meal. You always have room for a piece of this pie. It does take a little time so try mixing a little green crème de menthe with 7-Up and pouring over ice. This is a refreshing drink, especially good on a hot day. Now that you have had a sip of your drink, let's make the crumb crust for the pie.

Crumb Crust:
1 1/3 cups chocolate wafer crumbs

1/4 cup sugar
1/3 cup softened butter or margarine

Combine crumbs, sugar, and the butter. Mix well and press firmly over bottom and sides of a 9-inch pie pan. Bake at 375° for 8 minutes. Cool. Have a few sips and then you will be ready to make the filling.

Filling:
1 envelope unflavored gelatin
1/2 cup sugar
1/8 teaspoon salt
1/2 cup cold water
3 eggs, separated
1/4 cup green crème de menthe
1/4 cup white crème de cacao
1 cup whipping cream, whipped

Combine the gelatin, 1/4 cup sugar, and salt in the top of a double boiler. Add water and the egg yolks one at a time. Stir to blend well. Place over boiling water, stirring until the gelatin is dissolved and the mixture thickens slightly (about 5 minutes). Remove from water and stir in crème de menthe and crème de cacao. Chill, stirring occasionally, until the mixture is the consistency of unbeaten egg whites.

Beat egg whites stiff but not dry. Gradually add the remaining 1/4 cup sugar and beat until very stiff. Fold in the gelatin mixture and then the whipped cream. Pour into the crumb crust and chill 2 hours or overnight. If desired, garnish with whipped cream and/or chocolate crumbs.

If you don't have time to make the above pie, serve crème

de menthe over ice cream. It is very pretty layered in parfait glasses and topped with whipped cream. I keep some of these in my freezer just for unexpected guests.

Individual Cheesecakes

We bake these cherry-topped cheesecakes in muffin tins; this eliminates arguments over the size of servings. Now it is just how many does Dad get. You will find them ideal for picnics, too. Pour a little Cherry Heering into a cordial glass and get out your muffin tins. This should make 12 cheesecakes.

1 cup chocolate cookie crumbs
1 package softened cream cheese (8 ounces)
1/3 cup sugar
1 egg
2 teaspoons lemon juice
1 teaspoon apricot liqueur

Topping:
1/2 cup sugar
2 tablespoons cornstarch
1 can tart red cherries (1 pound)
2 tablespoons Cherry Heering

Make the topping first so that it has time to cool. Combine the sugar and cornstarch in a saucepan. Add the cherries with their syrup and the Cherry Heering. This is a good time for a sip. Cook and stir until the mixture comes to a boil and thickens. If you want a brighter red color, add a few drops of red food coloring. Set aside and let cool.

Fill muffin tins with paper liners and put a tablespoon of crushed cookie crumbs in each cup. We like chocolate, but any crisp cookie can be used. Have a sip and proceed to the filling. Beat together the cream cheese, sugar, egg, lemon juice, and apricot liqueur until smooth. Spoon into muffin tins and bake at 375° for 20 minutes or until set. Top with cherry sauce.

Kahlua Cream Puffs

Cream puffs are always a treat but more so with our Kahlua cream filling. I like to make a double batch of the cream puff shells and keep them in the freezer for unexpected guests. If you don't have time to make a filling try vanilla ice cream mixed with Kahlua or crème de menthe. It's a quick dessert that never fails to impress your friends. Mix a Kahlua Supreme to sip.

1 cup water
1/3 cup butter
1 cup sifted flour
2 eggs

Cream Filling:
1 package chocolate chips (8 ounces)
2 cups cream
2 tablespoons coffee liqueur

Take a sip of your drink as you bring butter and water to a boil in a saucepan. Have flour measured and ready to add. As soon as the mixture boils, remove from heat and stir in flour; beat vigorously with a wooden spoon until dough sticks together and comes away from the side of the pan. Add eggs one at a time and beat hard after adding each one. Drop by tablespoons onto a greased cookie sheet. Bake at 400° for 10 minutes. Reduce heat to 350° and bake for 25 minutes longer.

While cream puffs are baking have another sip and prepare the Kahlua cream filling. Combine the chocolate chips and cream in a saucepan. Heat slowly, stirring constantly until the chocolate melts. Remove from heat and stir in Kahlua. Pour into a bowl and chill 2 hours. Enjoy the rest of your drink. The mixture must be cold, then beat until stiff and thick. Fill cream puffs and chill at least one hour.

Mickey Finn Pineapple

Here is a dessert to top off your next luau. It is served in the pineapple shell and gives an authentic island feeling to your party. It is laced with crème de menthe for flavor and color.

1 large pineapple
1 pint orange, lemon, or lime sherbet
crème de menthe
mint sprigs

Sip on a crème de menthe on the rocks as you prepare this elegant dessert. Cut crown and bottom off the pineapple, slicing at least 1 inch down into the pineapple and save top for a decoration. With a long sharp knife, **cut** around the pineapple fruit and remove from the pineapple leaving about 1/2-inch thick shell. Dice the pineapple, discarding the tough center core. Have a sip and pack layers of pineapple and sherbet back into the shell. Cover with foil and freeze until sherbet is firm or until ready to serve. Remove from freezer 10 minutes before serving; cut into wedges and sprinkle with crème de menthe. Serve on a platter with the top in the center. Garnish with mint sprigs.

Orange Gems

This chocolate chip cookie with a subtle orange flavor disappears quickly with children or adults around. The prepared biscuit mix makes it a quick cookie to bake. A good time to make a week's supply is after dinner. It's also the best time to enjoy a glass of curacao. Take just one sip to start so you are still in the mood to make cookies. It won't take long.

3/4 cup brown sugar
1/4 cup shortening
1 egg
1 tablespoon orange juice
1 tablespoon orange curacao
1 1/2 cups biscuit mix
1/2 cup chopped pecans
1 cup chocolate chips

Cream sugar and shortening together. Add egg and orange juice and have a sip as you pour in the curacao. Stir in biscuit mix until well blended. Finish your drink and stir in the nuts and chocolate chips. Drop by teaspoons onto an ungreased cookie sheet. Bake at 375° for 10 minutes or until done.

Peaches and Cream Mold

This is an attractive summer dessert. If you are lucky enough to have a peach tree in your yard, you will want to make this a weekly dish during the peach season. I often sprinkle a little peach brandy over the peaches just before serving for a little added sparkle.

1 package mixed fruit flavored gelatin (3 ounces)
1 cup boiling water
1 cup sugar
1 package softened cream cheese (3 ounces)
1 cup cream, whipped
1 1/2 cups flaked coconut
2 teaspoons peach brandy
6 fresh peaches, peeled, sliced, and sugared

Dissolve the gelatin in boiling water. Cool slightly and pour yourself a glass of peach brandy to sip. Blend sugar and cream cheese; add the gelatin mixture and chill until it begins to thicken. Beat until thick and fluffy. Fold in whipped cream, coconut, and peach brandy. Spoon into a 2-quart ring mold and chill until firm. Unmold on a plate and spoon peaches in the center. To keep the peaches from turning dark, dip them in lemon juice as you peel and slice each one.

Rocky Road Cookies

Fill your cordial glass with crème de cacao and sip very slowly. This is a good cookie to make after dinner because the crème de cacao tastes best then.

1 cup sugar
2/3 cup shortening
2 eggs
1 tablespoon crème de cacao
2 squares unsweetened chocolate, melted
1/2 teaspoon salt
1/2 teaspoon baking powder
1 cup sifted flour
1/2 cup chopped walnuts
2 cups miniature marshmallows
1 cup chocolate chips, melted with 2 tablespoons butter

Cream the sugar and shortening together until smooth. Add the eggs one at a time, beating after each addition. Have a sip and stir in the crème de cacao and the melted chocolate. Add the dry ingredients and mix well. Stir in the nuts. Spread the batter into a greased 11 x 7 x 2" pan and bake at 350° for 25 minutes. This gives you time to finish your drink and maybe pour another. When done, remove the cookies from the oven and cover with the marshmallows. Pour the melted chocolate chips over all. Let it cool in the pan before cutting into squares.

Index

ALMOND
  with chicken, 150
  chocolate loaf cake, 130
  crab dip, 54
  oriental casserole, 62
  rice dressing, 153
  rice pudding, 118
  seafood casserole, 63, 64
APPETIZERS. See dips
  cheese ball, 148
  Cheese Log, 146
  crab cocktail, 132
  fruit, 39, 90
  onion bread, 20
  salmon spread, 147
  shrimp cocktail, 149
  Shrimp-Stuffed Mushrooms, 38
APPLE. See cider
  baked, 85
  gelatin salad, 75
  salad, 91
  stew, 79
APPLESAUCE
  cake, 101, 142
  muffins, 98

APRICOTS
  dried
    bread, 99
    fruit compote, 102
  fresh or canned
    dessert, 104
    gelatin salad, 92
    nut bread, 168
    steamed pudding, 107
  jam, coffee cake, 159
  nectar, cake, 171
ARTICHOKE
  French-fried, 30
  omelet, 46
Avocado, dip, 72

BACON
  bean casserole, 134
  Company Potatoes, 29
  garnish, 19, 68
BANANA
  ambrosia, 90
  bread, 116
  cake, 121
  flaming, 177
  frozen, 119

187

fruit cocktail, 39
gelatin salad, 42
BARBECUE
    chicken, 23
    chipped beef, 43
    spareribs, 93
Bean Sprouts, salad, 56
BEANS
    black-eyed peas, casserole, 134
    garbanzo, 77
    green, 68, 82
    kidney, 77, 82
    lima, 83
    with pork, 28, 72
BEEF. See hamburger
    chipped, 43
    corned, 57
    flank steak, 114
    liver, 24
    round steak, 26, 79, 133
    spareribs, 93
Beer, 19–36
Beets, pineapple, 166
BISCUIT MIX
    batter, 30
    bread, 20, 33, 168
    cookies, 183
    corn bread, 34
    dumplings, 50
    muffins, 98, 117
BRANDY
    dessert, 177
    soup, 161
    apple, waffles, 167
    apricot
        cake, 171
        coffee cake, 159
        French toast, 169
        nut bread, 168
    cherry, sauce, 163
    peach, gelatin dessert, 184
BREAD, QUICK. See muffins, nut bread
    banana, 116
    fritters, 137
    Hot Casserole, 33
    oatmeal biscuits, 43

Onion Crisps, 20
Spanish Corn Bread, 34
BREAD, YEAST
    dill, 32
    rolls, 31
Broccoli, casserole, 65, 81
Brussel Sprouts, soup, 73
BRUNCH SUGGESTIONS:
    Apple Brandy Waffles, 167
    Applewine Muffins, 98
    Apricot Royal, 102
    Apricot-Walnut Bread, 168
    Barbecued Chipped Beef, 43
    Bourbon-Molasses Doughnuts, 138
    Champagne Fruit Cocktail, 39
    Crabmeat-Artichoke Omelet, 46
    Double Scotch Muffins, 136
    Hangover Ambrosia, 90
    Island Muffins, 117
    Island Toast with Orange Curacao Syrup, 169
    Orange-Grapefruit-Champagne Salad, 41
    Spiked Ham and Cheese Sandwiches, 154
    Spiked Peach Coffee Cake, 159
BURGUNDY WINE
    casserole, 77, 81, 82
    cranberry chiffon pie, 86
    dip, 72
    sauce, 78
    soup, 73, 74
    stew, 79
    wineburgers, 77
BUTTERMILK
    chocolate cake, 130
    doughnuts, 138
Butterscotch, muffins, 136

Cabbage, casserole, 57
CAKE
    applesauce, 101
    banana, 121
    carrot, 105

cheese, 180
coffee, 159
cup, 173
date, 35
fruit, 129, 142, 143
gingerbread, 127
nut loaves, 130
pound, 171
rum, 128
short, 122, 124
strawberry, 109

CARROT
cake, 105
casserole, 49
with peas, 165
pudding, 120

Cashew, fried rice, 69

CASSEROLE
black-eyed peas, 134
carrots with rice, 49
chicken with dumplings, 155
chicken and peaches, 150
chicken with peas, 60
chicken and pork, 76
chicken with tomatoes, 59
corn, 96
eggplant, 84
green beans, 68
ham with hominy, 94
ham rolls, 67
hamburger and beans, 82
hot dog and rice, 23
meatball, 81
pork chop with noodles, 25
sausage and lima beans, 83
sausage and rice, 62
scallops and broccoli, 65
seafood, 63, 64
stew, 77
zucchini and corn, 48

CELERY
crab cocktail, 132
crab salad, 161
relish, 52
stuffing, 153

Chablis, casserole, 57, 61

CHAMPAGNE
appetizer, 38, 39

chicken, 45
dumplings, 50
gelatin dessert, 50
relish, 52
salad, 40, 41, 42
sherbet, 51
soup, 39
vegetable casserole, 48, 49

CHEESE
blue, appetizer, 148
cheddar
appetizer, 72, 148
bread, 33, 34
crab casserole, 151
ham casserole, 67, 94
lima bean and sausage casserole, 83
sandwich, 154
soup, 161
stuffed zucchini, 71
vegetable casserole, 49
cream
appetizer, 146, 148
cheesecake, 180
frosting, 106
fruit topping, 92
gelatin dessert, 184
mozzarella, casserole, 84
Parmesan
casserole, 59, 95, 150
fish, 164

CHERRIES
candied
cake, 143
cookies, 144
maraschino, cookies, 125, 172
sweet, ham sauce, 163
tart, cheescake, 180

Chianti, vegetable casserole, 68, 84

CHICKEN
barbecued, 23
with biscuits, 62
casserole, 60
with dumplings, 155
Mexican chicken, 59
with peaches, 150
with pork, 76
with rice, 45

190 / Sip and Stir

Chilies, corn bread, 34
CHINESE CASSEROLE
    crab, 61
    sausage and rice, 62
CHOCOLATE
  chips
    cake, 128
    cookies, 174, 183, 185
    cream filling, 181
    frozen bananas, 119
  cocoa
    apple cake, 101
    cookies, 126
  unsweetened
    cake, 130
    cookies, 175, 185
Christmas, wine jelly, 87
Cider, hard sauce, 168
Claret Wine, casserole, 81
COCONUT
    cookies, 125
    French toast, 169
    frosting, 122
    gelatin dessert, 123, 184
    muffins, 117
    shortcake, 124
Coffee, pudding, 140
COLD DUCK
    barbecue sauce, 43
    salad, 42
    stewed tomatoes, 47
COOKIES
  bar
    mint brownies, 175
    rocky road, 185
  drop
    bourbon, 137
    fruit, 144
    orange, 183
    sweet potato, 110
  rolled
    bourbon snaps, 139
    cherry balls, 172
    crème de cacao balls, 174
    rum balls, 126
    rum dums, 125
CORN
    bread, 34
    relish, 91
    tamale pie, 28
    vegetable casserole, 48, 96
CORN MEAL
    casserole, 28
    muffins, 170
    Spanish cornbread, 34
Cornish Hen, 153
COTTAGE CHEESE
    appetizer, 147
    bread, 32
    casserole, 81
    dumplings, 104
CRABMEAT
    casserole, 63, 64
    chowder, 55
    cocktail, 132
    dip, 54
    omelet, 46
    oriental, 61
    pilaf, 151
    salad, 161
CRANBERRY
    gelatin salad, 75
    jelly, 87
    pie, 86
CREAM, WHIPPED
    gelatin dessert, 106, 184
    gelatin salad, 162
    grasshopper pie, 178
    mocha pie, 177
Cream Puffs, 181
CRÈME DE MENTHE
    brownies, 175
    gelatin salad, 162
    grasshopper pie, 178
    peas and carrots, 165
CURACAO
    cookies, 183
    cupcakes, 173
    muffins, 170
    pie, 176
    syrup, 169

DATE
    cake, 35
    steamed pudding, 107

DESSERTS. See cookies, cake
  baked apples, 85
  cheesecake, 180
  cream puffs, 181
  dumplings, 50, 104
  frozen bananas, 119
  fruit, 177, 182
  fruit compote, 102
  gelatin, 42, 92, 106
  grape fluff, 50
  Margarita pie, 156
  peach mold, 184
  pineapple mint, 162
  sherbet, 51
  shortcake, 122, 124
  tarts, 157
DIPS
  crab, 54
  bean, 72
Doughnuts, 138
DRINKS
  Biarritz Cocktail, 176
  Gloom Chaser, 167
  Red Lion, 166
  Wine Cooler, 81
DUMPLINGS
  chicken, 155
  fruit, 104
  peach, 50

EGG
  crab omelet, 46
  Monte Cristo sandwich, 154
  hard cooked
    casserole, 95
    garnish, 55, 132
EGGPLANT
  casserole, 84
  stuffed, 97

FISH
  fillets, 164
  salmon, 66, 147
  swordfish, 152
  tuna, 95
Fondue, 19
Frankfurter, casserole, 23, 77
French Toast, 169

Fritters, rye, 137
FROSTING
  coconut, 121
  cream cheese, 106
  orange, 111
FRUIT
  candied
    cake, 129, 142, 143
    cookies, 144
  cocktail, trifle, 141
FRUIT WINE, 88–112
  apple
    cake, 101
    dessert, 106
    muffins, 98
    salad, 91
  apricot
    bread, 99
    dessert, 102, 104
    salad, 92
    steamed pudding, 107
  blackberry
    ambrosia, 90
    pudding, 103
  honey, barbecue sauce, 93
  loganberry, casserole, 76
  Madeira
    tuna pie, 95
    wine sauce, 111
  strawberry
    cake, 109
    pie, 108

Game Hens, 153
GELATIN
  desserts
    ambrosia, 90
    grape fluff, 50
    Hawaiian, 123
    lemon bisque, 106
    peach mold, 184
  salad
    fruit, 42, 75, 92
    grapefruit, 41, 42
    orange-champagne, 40
    pineapple mint, 162
GIN
  cheese ball, 148

chicken and dumplings, 155
crab pilaf, 151
sandwich, 154
Gingerbread, 127
GRAND MARNIER
   crab salad, 161
   fish casserole, 164
   peach dumplings, 50
   vegetables, 166, 167
GRAPE
   chicken, 45
   dessert, 50
GRAPEFRUIT
   ambrosia, 90
   salad, 41, 42
Green Pepper, relish, 52
Grits, pilaf, 135
Gumdrop, cake, 142

HAM
   beans, 28
   casserole, 67, 94
   with cherry sauce, 163
   with rum sauce, 113
   sandwiches, 154
HAMBURGER
   bean casserole, 82
   meatballs, 74, 81
   soup, 73, 74
   spaghetti sauce, 78
   stew, 77
   tamale pie, 28
   wineburgers, 77
Hard Sauce, 167
Hominy, casserole, 94
HONEY
   acorn squash, 115
   cookies, 172
Hors d'oeuvre. See appetizers

Irish Whiskey, pudding, 140

Jelly, wine, 87

KAHLUA
   cream filling, 181
   mocha pie, 177

LEFTOVERS
   cake, 141
   French bread, 19, 161
   rice, 23, 49
Lemon, dessert, 106

Macaroon, dessert, 123
MARINADE
   fish, 152
   steak, 114
MARSHMALLOWS
   gelatin salad, 42, 92
   mocha pie, 177
   rocky road cookies, 185
MEXICAN
   Chicken Acapulco, 59
   Spanish Corn Bread, 34
   Tamale Pie, 28
   Tostada Bean Dip, 72
Mincemeat, muffins, 170
MOLASSES
   doughnuts, 138
   fritters, 137
   gingerbread, 127
MUFFINS
   applewine, 98
   double scotch, 136
   island, 117
   mincemeat, 170
MUSHROOMS
   chicken casserole, 60, 62, 155
   ham casserole, 94
   meatball casserole, 57, 81
   pilaf ring, 135
   seafood casserole, 63, 64
   spaghetti sauce, 78

NOODLES
   casserole, 25, 81
   Chinese, casserole, 64
   with stew, 79
NUT BREAD
   apricot, 99, 168
   pumpkin, 100
Nuts. See individual names

OATMEAL
  biscuits, 44
  cookies, 137, 174
OLIVES
  chicken casserole, 59
  garnish, 70
  sausage casserole, 83
  tamale pie, 28
Onion, soup, 161
ORANGE
  ambrosia, 90
  cookies, 183
  crab salad, 161
  cupcakes, 173
  frosting, 111
  fruit cocktail, 39
  gelatin salad, 40, 41
  meat marinade, 114
  nut bread, 99
  pie, 176
  rhubarb soup, 39
  rum sauce, 113
  tarts, 157

PASTRY
  chocolate crumb, 178
  pretzel crumb, 156
PEACH
  chicken casserole, 150
  coffee cake, 159
  dumplings, 50
  gelatin dessert, 184
  shortcake, 124
PEAS
  with carrots, 165
  chicken casserole, 60
PECAN
  cookies, 144, 183
  cupcakes, 173
  flaming bananas, 177
  muffins, 98
  nut bread, 99
PIE
  cranberry chiffon, 86
  grasshopper, 178
  Margarita, 156
  mocha, 177

  orange-cocoa, 176
  strawberry-lemonade, 108
PILAF
  casserole, 151
  grits, 135
PINEAPPLE
  ambrosia, 90
  baked beans, 28
  beets, 166
  cranberry salad, 75
  curacao syrup, 170
  filled with sherbet, 182
  fruit salad, 40, 42, 92
  marinade, 114
  mint salad, 162
  rum sauce, 113
  shortcake, 122
  topping, 123
PORK. See ham
  chicken casserole, 76
  oriental dish, 61
  pork chop casserole, 25
  sausage
    casserole, 82, 83
    eggplant stuffing, 97
    oriental dish, 62
  spareribs, 93
PORT
  cranberry salad, 75
  ham sauce, 163
POTATO CHIPS
  bread, 20
  sandwiches, 154
POTATOES
  Company Potatoes, 29
  instant, 70
Poultry. See chicken
PRETZEL
  garnish, 66
  pie crust, 156
PUDDING
  berry tapioca, 103
  Irish Whiskey, 140
  rice, 118
  steamed, 107, 120
Pumpkin, nut bread, 100

194 / Sip and Stir

Raspberry, pudding, 103
Red Wines, 72–87
RELISH
    apple-corn, 91
    kraut, 52
Rhine Wine, potatoes, 70
RICE
    bean casserole, 28
    carrot casserole, 49
    Crab Pilaf, 151
    fried, 69
    hot dog casserole, 23
    pudding, 118
    sausage casserole, 62
    seafood casserole, 63
    Stuffed Zucchini, 71
    stuffing, 153
    wild, 45, 63
Rhubarb, soup, 39
Rolls. See bread
Rum, 113–31
Rye, fritters, 137

SALAD
    bean sprout, 56
    citrus gelatin, 40, 41, 42
    corn relish, 91
    crab, 161
    cranberry, 75
    fruit, 39, 90
    fruit gelatin, 42, 92, 162
    kraut relish, 52
    stuffed apples, 85
Salmon. See fish
Sandwich, ham and cheese, 154
SAUCE
    barbecue, 93
    cherry, 163
    pineapple, 122
    rum, 113
    spaghetti, 78
    wine, 111
Sauerkraut, relish, 52
SAUTERNE WINE
    chicken, 60, 62
    crab chowder, 55
    fried rice, 69
    seafood casserole, 64

Scallops, casserole, 65
Scotch, muffins, 136
Seafood. See individual names
SHERBET
    filled pineapple, 182
    Pink Champagne, 51
SHERRY
    cake, 105
    casserole, 94, 96
    pumpkin bread, 100
    stuffed eggplant, 97
    sweet potato cookies, 110
SHORTCAKE
    peach, 124
    pineapple, 122
SHRIMP
    casserole, 63, 64
    cocktail, 149
    stuffed mushrooms, 38
Snack. See appetizers
SOUP
    burgundy burger, 73, 74
    crab chowder, 55
    onion cheese, 161
    rhubarb, 39
    spinach, 21
    vegetable, 22
SOUR CREAM
    cake, 128
    chicken casserole, 150
    frosting, 121
    gravy, 26
    onion bread, 20
    shrimp cocktail, 149
Sparkling Wines, 37–53
SPICE
    cookies, 137, 139
    date cake, 35
SPINACH
    casserole, 23, 67
    fried rice, 69
    soup, 21
STRAWBERRY
    ambrosia, 90
    cake, 109
    fruit cocktail, 39
    pie, 108
    soup, 39

Squash. *See* acorn
Stew, 77, 79
SWEET POTATO
  cookies, 110
  orange, 167
SYRUP
  hard cider, 168
  orange, 170

Tamale Pie, 28
Tapioca, pudding, 103
Tarts, 157
Tequila, Margarita Pie, 156
TOMATO
  beans, 28
  casserole, 59, 133
  eggplant, 97
  fish, 164
  potato dish, 29
  rice, 69
  soup, 55, 73
  spaghettic sauce, 78
  stewed, 47
Tuna, pie, 95

Vegetables. *See* individual names
VODKA
  cheese log, 146
  chicken casserole, 150

game hens, 153
salmon spread, 147
shrimp cocktail, 149
swordfish, 152
tarts, 157

Waffles, 167
WALNUTS
  brownies, 175
  cake, 35, 142, 143
  cookies, 110, 139, 172, 185
  nut breads, 100, 168
  pudding, 140
  steamed pudding, 107
  waffles, 167
WATER CHESTNUTS
  cabbage and meatballs, 57
  salad, 56
  seafood casserole, 64
Whiskey, 132-45
White Wines, 54-71

YOGURT
  muffins, 117
  pie, 108

ZUCCHINI
  casserole, 48
  stuffed, 71

WIDENER UNIVERSITY-WOLFGRAM LIBRARY

CIR TX726.M37 1973
Sip and stir

3 3182 00289 3276

TX 726 .M37 1973
Meek, Joanne.
Sip and stir